QUEEN MARGARET UNIVERSITY

100 304 829

Withdrawn from
Queen Margaret University Library

Designing Mind-Friendly Environments

D1381652

Withdrawn from
Queen Margaret University Library
QUEEN MARGARET UNIVERSITY LRC

of related interest

Sensory Perceptual Issues in Autism and
Asperger Syndrome, Second Edition
Different Sensory Experiences – Different Perceptual Worlds
Olga Bogdashina
Foreword by Manuel Casanova
ISBN 978 1 84905 673 1
eISBN 978 1 78450 179 2

Living Sensationally
Understanding Your Senses
Winnie Dunn
ISBN 978 1 84310 915 0
eISBN 978 1 84642 733 6

Design for Nature in Dementia Care
Garuth Chalfont
ISBN 978 1 84310 571 8
eISBN 978 1 84642 676 6
Bradford Dementia Group Good Practice Guides

Designing Mind-Friendly Environments

Design and Architecture for Everyone

Steve Maslin, RIBA, FSI, NRAC

Foreword by Zoe Mailloux,
OTD, OTR/L, FAOTA

Jessica Kingsley Publishers
London and Philadelphia

First published in Great Britain in 2022 by Jessica Kingsley Publishers
An Hachette Company

1

Copyright © Steve Maslin, Dip Arch, RIBA, FSI, NRAC 2022
Foreword copyright © Zoe Mailloux, OTD, OTR/L, FAOTA 2022

All rights reserved. No part of this publication may be reproduced, stored
in a retrieval system, or transmitted, in any form or by any means without
the prior written permission of the publisher, nor be otherwise circulated
in any form of binding or cover other than that in which it is published and
without a similar condition being imposed on the subsequent purchaser.

A CIP catalogue record for this title is available from the
British Library and the Library of Congress

ISBN 978 1 78592 142 1
eISBN 978 1 78450 414 4

Printed and bound in Great Britain by CPI Group

Jessica Kingsley Publishers' policy is to use papers that are natural,
renewable and recyclable products and made from wood grown in
sustainable forests. The logging and manufacturing processes are expected
to conform to the environmental regulations of the country of origin.

Jessica Kingsley Publishers
Carmelite House
50 Victoria Embankment
London EC4Y 0DZ

www.jkp.com

Contents

Acknowledgements 13

Disclaimer 15

Foreword by Zoe Mailloux, OTD, OTR/L, FAOTA 16

Preface 18
The need for this book   18
My experience   19
Reflections on my experience   19
Audiences   21
Seek specialist advice   22
Universal relevance   23
A note on scope   23

Introduction 25

Section A: Connecting Different 'Worlds'

1. Definitions and Voice 31
   Needs and aspirations   32
   Models of disability   32
   Divisive use of language   34
   Chosen terminology   34
   Voice and invisibility   35

2. Learning from People on the Autistic Spectrum 36
   Autism   36
   Universal experiences   37
   Childhood experiences   38
   Dementia   39
   Brain/nerve trauma/damage   39
   Physiological factors   40
   Dyslexia and dyscalculia   41
   Dyspraxia   41
   Learning difficulties   42

Migraines, epilepsy, phobias, etc. 43
Mental illness 46
Behavioural difficulties 47
Medication/drugs 48
Compound neurological experiences 48
Family, friends and support workers 49

3. Learning from OT, Psychology, UX and Inclusive Design . . . 51
Occupational therapy (OT) 51
Psychology: scientific research 52
Service design 52
Inclusive design and access consultancy 53

4. Design as Social Prescribing. 54
In the workplace 55
In education 55
In retail 55
In custody 56

5. Prescription to Commissioning 57
Intervention in context 58
Finding a voice 58
Finding confidence 59
Seeking allies 59
Strategy 61
Utilizing expertise 62
Project briefs 62
Proportionality 63

6. For Whom or With Whom? 65
Engagement, co-production and service design 65
Inclusive engagement 67
Avoid 'fluffy' engagement 69

Section B: The Human Experience

7. Diversity. 73
Envelope of need 75

8. Stress 77
Stress as indicator 77
Indicators of stress 78

9. Sensory Processing. 80
Mind: brain with senses 80
Our senses 81
Theoretical basis 83
Universal application 84
Application within environments 85

10. Emotion, Meaning and Metaphor.   87
    Avoiding confusion   88

11. Reasoning, Learning and Understanding.   91
    Perception   91
    Language, information and communication   92

12. Rest and Sleep   94
    Control and choice   94

Section C: Contextual Experience

13. Mind and Body in Context   99
    Sensory deprivation   99
    Sensory overload   101
    Other dimensions   102
    Context phobias and phenomena   103

14. Spatial Context. 104
    Auditory ingredients   104
    Visual ingredients   104
    Respiratory ingredients   105
    Aromatic ingredients   105
    Gustatory ingredients   105
    Tactile ingredients   106
    Proprioceptive and vestibular ingredients   106
    Thermal ingredients   109
    The chronometric ingredient   109
    The natural world   110
    Choice   110

15. Social Context 111
    The social world   111
    Mirroring and communication   112
    Choice of space   113
    Space bubbles and proxemics   114

16. Comfort and Activity 116
    Movement   116
    Furniture   117
    Facilities   118
    Choice of opportunity   118

17. Acoustics 119
    Pervasive sound   119
    Communication   120
    Singing and music   120
    Choice of acoustics: calm and stimulating   121
    Components of acoustics   122
    Assistive technology   125

18. **Lighting** 127
 Beyond illumination 127
 Choice of lighting: calm and stimulus 128
 Natural light 128
 Artificial light 129
 Light where one needs it 130
 Transition and external lighting 131
 Light and navigation 131
 Lighting problems 132

19. **Surfaces** 134
 Form and space perception 134
 Auditory surface perception 134
 Tactile surface perception 135
 Visual surface perception 136
 Specific surface considerations 141

20. **Tastes, Smells and Air Quality** 143
 Tasting one's environment 143
 Smelling and breathing in our environment 144
 Implications for design 145

21. **Temperature** 146
 Thermal comfort 146
 Air movement 147
 Implications for design 147

22. **The Natural World** 148
 Oxygen and temperature 148
 Daylight and views 148
 Multisensory world 149
 Biophilia 150
 Biophilic communities? 152
 Biomimicry 152
 Implications for design 152
 What could the results of improvements be? 153

23. **Time and Memory** 154
 Time 154
 Memory 154
 Implications for design 156

24. **Navigation, Place and Wayfinding** 157
 Wayfinding 157
 Welcome and convenience 158
 Signage 159
 Multisensory needs 160
 Pre- and on-arrival information 161
 Symbols 162

Enabling information	163
Points to note	164

25. Spatial Choice, Permission and Security 166
Choice 166
Security 167
Permission 170
Workplaces 170
Hospital, health and social care 171
Exhibitions 172
Custodial environments 172

26. Communication 173

Section D: Different Environments

27. Landscape and Urban 177
Context 177
Multiple stimuli 177
Navigation 178
Security 178
Design opportunities 178

28. Transport 180
Transition 180
Quiet spaces 181
Informative environments 181
Design criteria and opportunities 181

29. Education 183
Transfer of information 183
Diverse learning styles 183
Design criteria and opportunities 184

30. Health and Social Care. 186
Wellbeing or stress? 186
Health and social care workers 187
Design criteria and opportunities 188

31. Workplaces 190
Productivity 190
Design opportunities 191

32. Places of Worship 193
Why are you going? 193
Historic example 193
Designing places of worship for the future 195

33. Communal 197
Community and individuality 197

34. **Cultural and Civic** 199
    Ingredients and design opportunities   199

35. **Leisure and Sports** 202
    Ingredients and design opportunities   202

36. **Food and Drink** 204
    Ingredients   204
    Design opportunities   205

37. **Retail** 208
    Hunting, foraging and design opportunities   208

38. **Hospitality** 211
    Sensory rest and stimulation   211
    Design criteria and opportunities   212

39. **Industrial and Military** 213
    Critical situations   213
    Design considerations and opportunities   214

40. **Judicial and Custodial** 216
    Restorative or punitive?   216
    Custodial design   217
    Court design   218

41. **Domestic** 220
    Secure and comfortable   220

Section E: Getting Serious

42. **Facilities Management** 225
    Design for operability   226
    Putting forward a case   226
    Joined-up thinking   227
    Sustainability   227
    Resilience   228
    Occupants   228
    Information management   229

43. **Safeguarding of Wellbeing** 230
    Accountability   230
    Wellbeing   230
    Whereabouts   231
    External threats   231
    Curtilages   232
    Natural surveillance   232
    Extreme situations   233
    Safe space safeguards   234
    Unintended consequences   238
    Wider impacts   238

44. Fire and Emergencies 240
   Universal benefit   240
   Accentuated neurological need   240
   Evacuation plans   241
   Planning   242
   Design and management   243
   Watch points   246
   Fire and emergencies summary   248

Summary 249

Author Biography 251

List of Figures 254

References 256

Endnotes 263

Index 268

Acknowledgements

I would especially like to acknowledge my immediate family who have provided me with the time and context in which I could pursue the writing of this book. Thank you, Christine, and thank you too, Hannah and Joseph, for also modelling for many of the photographs contained within this book. Thank you also to Hannah for assisting with processing some of the images too.

It would also be apt to give thanks to both my parents, Roger and Meg, and to my teachers, since without their help and encouragement I could so easily have struggled to get to the point of writing this book. The teachers that stand out in my mind are Mr Webb (my head teacher who listened and learnt about dyslexia), Mr Elliott (my classroom teacher who encouraged me) and Mrs Mayo-Smith (my English teacher who provided me with extra tuition), but there are many others whom I owe my thanks to also.

Since portions of what I have written are derived from earlier writings (listed in the Author Biography), I would like to acknowledge the following organizations for providing me the opportunity to put my early thoughts down:

- The Centre for Accessible Environments, publisher of 'A Favourite Building: The New Room, Bristol' (Maslin 2005)

- Workplace Law Group, publisher of 'Fire and Disability 2008 – Special Report', edited by Claire Fuller (Maslin, 2008)

- The Nature of Cities (TNOC), publisher of 'What Are We Trying to Accomplish with Biophilic Cities? What Are Ambitious Goals and Targets, and Measures of Success?' (Maslin, 2017)

- my former employers, Stride Treglown.

A shout-out also goes to my current employers, Atkins, who take a positive stand with regard to people's neurodiversity, foster an internal neurodiversity network and have embarked on a journey towards greater inclusion, including acknowledging the contribution that diverse staff bring to a business and exploring better ways of recruiting people with neuro-atypical minds.

I would also like to acknowledge a whole range of people for those inspiring conversations or written exchanges that helped me on my journey (many of whom get a mention in this book and are referenced in the Bibliography). In particular, I would like to thank Dr Zoe Mailloux, Adjunct Associate Professor of Occupational Therapy at Thomas Jefferson University, for agreeing to write the Forward to this book. I would like to thank her for her enthusiasm for the role that architecture could have in delivering mind-friendly environments. I would also like to thank neuropsychologist Dr Ute Leonards, Professor of Neuropsychology at the University of Bristol,[1] for reading through an earlier draft of my book, providing me with feedback and drawing me in to her world of psychology whilst valuing my thoughts as an architect.

Occupational therapist Dr Winnie Dunn, Distinguished Professor of Occupational Therapy at the University of Missouri, should also get a mention for her encouragement and her inspirational book *Living Sensationally: Understanding Your Senses* (Dunn, 2007). Thank you too to occupational psychologist Dr Craig Knight, UX designer Alistair Somerville and sensory lab owner Steven J. Orfield for conversations that have contributed to my thinking.

Last, and by no means least, as a Christian, it would also be inconsistent of me not to acknowledge the role that I believe God has had in directing my paths and to acknowledge that it is His natural creation that enables the facilitation of mind-friendly environments. I would not want to pretend either that just enabling mind-friendly environments is all our minds need. Therefore, I wish to thank my Lord and Saviour, Jesus, the Prince of Peace, for so wonderfully expressing God's love, which I have found so essential for our ultimate wellbeing.

Disclaimer

Whilst it is sad to have to spell this bit out, it is necessary for legal reasons to make it clear that:

- opinions expressed in this book are given in good faith and are solely for the purpose of prompting thought and discussion, for which readers take their own responsibility

- reading and acting on this book is not a substitute for advice obtained through formal professional appointments directly with architects, access consultants or other professionals

- without the presence of any formal appointment, the author and the businesses/organizations with which he is and has been associated accept no liability for the decisions or actions of readers and/or others acting on their behalf.

Foreword

As an occupational therapist interested in the powerful influence
that one's environment exerts on all aspects of human life, I am
thrilled to introduce *Designing Mind-Friendly Environments*. That my
path would cross with architect and author Steve Maslin in such
a significant way has been fortuitous, but perhaps not surprising.
In fact, the very name of my profession, 'occupational therapy',
was coined by an architect, Edward Barton,[1] who gathered with
a small founding group to form the National Society for the
Promotion of Occupational Therapy at Consolation House in New
York over one hundred years ago. Occupational therapy, and our
profession's dedication to helping 'people across the lifespan to do
the things they want and need to do through the therapeutic use
of daily activities (occupations)'[2] is inextricable from environmental
considerations.

As research assistant to Dr A. Jean Ayres,[3] the founder of
sensory integration theory and practice, I was fortunate to have
a first-hand view of the impact of her groundbreaking work.
Steve's incorporation of sensory integration principles into
design considerations would impress and please Dr Ayres. His
understanding and application of the ways in which *all* the senses
guide and impact our response to environments is exquisite. Steve's
description of his own learning struggles is not unlike those Dr
Ayres herself experienced. Their revelations are reflective of the
ways that all humans process and understand best – that is, through
personal experience. The fact that Steve so strongly and clearly
promotes a universal approach to mind-friendly environments is a

testament to his awareness that everyone lives, learns, plays and works better when the environment supports all.

In *Designing Mind-Friendly Environments*, Steve provides an exquisite and comprehensive case for universal, inclusive design, which not only considers, but actually takes joy in human diversity. Alongside his accomplishments in the field of architecture and design, Steve pairs his curiosity and mastery of complex topics from sensory integration to proxemics to give us this exceptional roadmap for adapting and developing environments that will support productivity, comfort, creativity and successful engagement for all.

What a promising future we will have if the concepts Steve outlines in a scholarly and credible way in *Designing Mind-Friendly Environments* become required reading for a multitude of professionals, not only in architecture and design but also in education, organizational psychology, business management and, of course, the health fields, including occupational therapy. I know that this book will become one of my go-to resources and recommendations.

Dr Zoe Mailloux OTD, OTR/L, FAOTA, Adjunct
Assistant Professor of Occupational Therapy
*Department of Occupational Therapy, Thomas
Jefferson University, Philadelphia, PA, USA*
Founder: Sensory Aware and Friendly Environments (SAFE)
Co-Founder: Collaborative for Ayres Sensory Integration (CLASI)

Preface

The need for this book

Time and time again we learn of people developing stress responses to environments. Yet have you ever wondered why means for avoiding this seem not widely known amongst those who commission and design buildings? The irony is that if you talk to some people from within therapeutic, medical, teaching and social services fields, you learn of knowledge that is being applied as interventions within these disciplines that could perhaps be applied within the environments in which people are themselves endeavouring to function, with longer-lasting results.

Although there is much information on this subject out there, you have to hunt for it! Apart from a few exceptions, there appears to be a significant gap between the therapeutic world and the world of built-environment design when it comes to engaging with people's neurological needs – especially when it comes to inclusive design information that it would be reasonable to expect to be accessed by designers. Even then, the books that are out there are either written with a specific neurological condition in mind or are from a more philosophical frame of reference. Few books, it seems, take the approach that project commissioners, architects and designers have something to learn from a diverse range of people who have accentuated neurological experiences so that they might then commission and design environments that are more mind friendly for everyone. Hence the need for this book and my efforts towards establishing 'Design for the Mind' guidance at the British Standards Institute.[1]

My experience

As you will gather from my qualifications (as set out in the Author Biography at the end of this book), I am not a neuroscientist, psychologist or the like. I am quite simply an architect and access consultant who has had an unusual career path, who has identified an information gap and who has sought to acquire knowledge through conversing with different disciplines to fill that gap. My expertise is in providing inclusive, universal, people-centred and user experience-informed design advice. My accreditation for this work comes from the UK's National Register of Access Consultants (NRAC).

What led me to explore this subject was my own personal and practical experience gained whilst working with adults with learning difficulties during the '90s. To give you an idea of how this experience came my way:

- I was late learning to speak; thought to have had a hearing impairment; had hearing, eye and speech tests; found not to have any physical reasons for my difficulties; and was eventually diagnosed with dyslexia during the early '70s.

- I worked as a part-time and supply group worker for local social services over a period of six years in and around Bristol in the UK, working in well over ten different centres and regularly in specific centres. People I worked with had a variety of needs, including moderate to severe learning difficulties, autism, 'behavioural' difficulties and profound and multiple related needs.

I also currently facilitate a group activity (consisting of prayer, Bible reading and worship) with a group of friends who have moderate to severe learning difficulties.

Reflections on my experience

One of the founders of the British Dyslexia Association (BDA)[2] Marion Welchman[3] once referred to me as one of the 'early boys' because I was assessed as having dyslexia whilst pioneering work **about dyslexia was being done** in the City of Bath **in the early** '70s, and soon after the BDA was set up in 1972. The educational psychologist who assessed me for dyslexia, Mr Green, identified that whilst I had particular difficulties associated with dyslexia, I had advanced spatial reasoning abilities for my age. Little wonder that I ended up as an architect! Even so, few in my early years would have thought that I could go on to gain graduate, postgraduate and professional qualifications, let alone write a book!

For me, personally, my dyslexia diagnosis helped explain factors beyond assumptions about intellect or physical causes. My mother was told by my infant school head teacher, prior to my dyslexia diagnosis, that 'You have two sons. One will go far; don't expect too much of the other one.' My younger brother Paul did indeed go far, and he is now a doctor practicing as a GP. His older brother (me) was the 'other one'! When our younger sister, Sue, came onto the scene, she too outperformed me when it came to language – beating me at Scrabble every time we played despite being five years younger! Indeed, both my brother and sister have exceptional abilities and qualities.

Having embarked on a journey of discovery, I now better understand the significance of the early observation that others had made about what they thought was associated with my hearing or my intellect. This is because as a child I found it difficult to decipher and decode what others were saying and what I was reading and to then encode what I wanted to say or write in reply. I now realize that my both my difficulties and abilities could be more fully explained by the neurological processes of sensory processing and integration.

However, the perception that I might have had a hearing impairment was quite astute. At school, you would have found me positioning myself at the front of classrooms at risk of being called a 'keener'. This was so that I would have the greatest opportunity to hear the teacher clearly so that I could then decipher what they were saying. It is also worth mentioning that my difficulties and my associated lack of confidence (which accompanied me finding communication difficult) led to me being bullied at school, as I found it difficult to relate to my peers, and coincided with other health issues. I mention this as the complexity and multidimensional aspects of a person's experience are always worth bearing in mind.

Given my auditory processing difficulties, it is no wonder I still find extraneous noise or poor and overly reverberant acoustics difficult! Whilst not quite painful, I can nevertheless find such environments neurologically stressful and detrimental to my ability to think clearly – let alone detrimental to my ability to work out what others are saying. For others, their difficulties will be similar or different to mine, and yet as you read this book you should hopefully discover an underlying unifying thread of sensory processing and integration insights that we can all relate to in one way or another!

Audiences

As you will have gathered from the book title, my pursuit is to enable better commissioning and design practice when it comes to people's neurological needs. I have endeavoured to identify and seek to address key target audiences so that these audiences might themselves be enabled to help one another:

1. **The most poignant audience** includes those who may benefit most from the application of this knowledge. They may struggle to function in certain environments, and they may wish to learn of ways to adapt their environment, find more conducive environments and/or point decision-makers towards means of addressing the issues that they face.

2. **The most pivotal audience** includes those who may consider themselves as informed – such as those within the therapeutic, medical, teaching and social services communities – who may want to influence commissioning and design processes and yet lack the confidence and knowledge as how to do this.

3. **The most essential audience** are those who will have the greatest impact on environments, who are commissioning a project, receiving a project brief or are going to manage an environment and who may be less aware of the relevance of the mind to design. These include commissioners, project managers, architects, landscape architects, designers, contractors, facilities managers and others in the supply chain.

Seek specialist advice

My plea to fellow architects and designers and to the therapeutic, teaching, medical and social services communities is to not assume that you can pursue the briefing and design process without the input of someone like me to collaborate with and advise you. Too often, I and fellow consultants with knowledge in this area see others endeavouring to undertake the process of designing without us, and without the stakeholders with whom we would like clients and design teams to engage.

Yes, this book should help you – but it is not intended to replace years of acquired knowledge and experience. This applies not only to experience with the subject of this book but also includes experience with the equally important physical, auditory and visual needs that people have in the built environment, for which registered access consultants like me are equipped to advise on. In the UK, the recognized body for accrediting access consultants is the National Register of Access Consultants.

If you possess only people-facing knowledge or technical knowledge, you will need someone with both these hard and soft skills to bridge the gap. Registered access consultants span between these realms of knowledge that others can easily gloss over, misinterpret or lack the confidence to apply. Even then, those with in-depth knowledge of people's neurological needs are a relatively unusual 'breed' within access consultancy at the moment. So, *please* utilize the knowledge of appropriately experienced registered access consultants when embarking on a project...and preferably well before you set out on the design process!

Universal relevance

Please do not think that this book is only about designing for people with particularly accentuated needs or only about specialist/supportive environments. It is as much about the design of environments in general and design to the benefit of everyone, with as much relevance to public environments and civic, retail and work places as it has to schools, hospitals and other even more specialist environments. As such, the book will look at different environments and make observations accordingly.[4]

A note on scope

Beyond this brief mention here, some may wonder why the subjects of electromagnetic hyper-sensitivity (EHS) (with regard to non-ionizing radiation at non-thermal levels) and multiple chemical sensitivities (MCS) are not directly addressed within the main body of the book. Not wishing to diminish the potential significance of these subjects as research and understanding develops (not least because there could hypothetically be some sensory processing aspects to these experiences and because there is precautionary government advice on devices that emit non-ionizing radiation at non-thermal levels), I have chosen not to go into these subjects in detail in this book, other than to refer to these subjects of concern at this point. Admittedly, this is because, whilst there are significant protagonists, there are is also significant scepticism surrounding these subjects, and I did not wish to make the job of persuading readers of the significance of what I am currently writing any harder.

For those concerned, however, the World Health Organization's website devotes several pages to electromagnetic fields and makes mention of both EHS and MCS.[5] For those wishing to hear a protagonist's view on EHS, Dr Erica Mallery-Blythe, MD, has a short online Vimeo video presentation on the subject.[6] For those wishing to read a critical take on the subject, then the current Wikipedia page on EHS[7] takes a sceptical standpoint.

Introduction

Although some people assume that the realm of the mind lacks tangibility, when it comes to designing environments, on the contrary, there is much about mind-friendly environments that is very tangible! As stated in the Preface, time and time again people develop stress responses to environments. When reading this book, you should hopefully see that when considering people's neurological needs, human-centric design should revolve around providing choice within environments in which diverse people can find a space in which they might function best at any given time.

It may also help readers to know that this book is written with a predominantly lateral, joined-up, systems-thinking approach, akin to the approach espoused by the Schumacher Institute for Sustainable Systems. In other words, it is not simply a linear piece of writing. Systems thinking takes a roundtable, interdisciplinary approach where engagement with different perspectives is essential. Since I am taking account of the perspective of users, designers and operators of environments, you may perceive that the book has more than one 'voice'. This is intentional. Readers are encouraged to engage in a similar way. If readers would like to undertake joined-up, systems thinking for their project, then please contact me or the Schumacher Institute for Sustainable Systems in Bristol, UK.[1]

Designing Mind-Friendly Environments is therefore written in order to enable mind-focused individuals, professionals and organizations to communicate with project commissioners, architects and designers, and then to enable project teams with specialist support (from individuals such as me) to incorporate mind-friendly principles into every project brief – both for existing and for new environments.

Please note that it is not my intent that designers create bland environments in response to this book but that they create environments that can be *enjoyed by all.* In other words:

> It is about enabling choice within environments, in which both joy and calm can be found, and enabling the ingredients that contribute to a mind-friendly environment to be orchestrated into the most elegant of architecture, urban realms and landscapes.

Whilst there are specialist environments that can be designed with particular attention to specific neurological conditions, the underlying principle of *Designing Mind-Friendly Environments* is to convey that it is possible to design mind-friendly environments, whatever the building and purpose is, in order that far more people can use different environments more effectively, whether they have a particular condition or not. By referring to specific experiences that people have, this book will simply be aiming to highlight some of the issues. Please note, therefore, that whilst much of the learning comes as a result of the experiences of people on the autistic spectrum, people living with dementia and other people with accentuated neurological experiences, this subject is relevant to everyone. As such:

> This book is based on the premise of the universal design principle that we should design inclusively and for everyone.

Nevertheless, *Designing Mind-Friendly Environments* should also help connect therapeutic, medical, teaching and social services disciplines (working with people with particular needs) with the built-environment design and commissioning world. It should also provide material for those with specific neurological experiences and their support networks as a means of drawing the attention of decision-makers to the issues and highlighting how these issues can cause other people problems as well. This is because whilst people will have different neurological needs, many of the underlying issues and design principles have a sufficiently similar starting place for a conversation to begin. This should then help decision-makers to discover the wider benefits of mind-friendly environments as well as how these issues can affect them too!

Designing Mind-Friendly Environments should also help human resources, customer services, equalities officers and facilities managers to gain insights into the diverse user experience of the people using the environments for which they are responsible.

So that readers might find greater ease in reading and digesting the contents, chapters are relatively short and organized within the following five sections:

- **Section A – Connecting Different 'Worlds'** will emphasize sources from whom insight and knowledge can be found and the importance of engagement between different parties in order to effect change.

- **Section B – The Human Experience** will explore aspects of the human experience, such as stress, and begin to unfold the relevance of the environment, prior to the core (and following section) of the book.

- **Section C – Contextual Experience** (the core of the book) will further explore the connection between our minds and our surroundings – drawing substantially on sensory integration theory and related studies.

- **Section D – Different Environments** (the culmination of the book) will focus on different environment types (external and internal) with particular attention to the principal activities of such environments and the neurological needs and anticipated benefits that should go with each environment.

- **Section E – Getting Serious** will look at how environments can either help or hinder the management of operations, wellbeing, safeguarding, safety and emergencies.

Connecting Different 'Worlds'

This section seeks to do some 'silo busting' and joined-up, systems thinking in order to enable readers to approach mind-friendly environments in a more universal way.

1

Definitions and Voice

Whilst we need a universal approach to achieving mind-friendly environments, language is a big part of achieving a more universal understanding.

For many, the realm of the mind has been a taboo subject – a result of fear and lack of knowledge. Consequently, many societies have been ill-equipped to talk about the subject. This is in part because we know that words are powerful, having the potential to provoke negative reactions through triggering that which we find most sensitive. This is especially the case when it comes to the mind. Therefore, every effort has been made to use well-considered words in this book.

No one likes to be offended. Similarly, few people want to give offence. Consequently, we all need to allow for *no offence to be intended* – despite the words used. If we look for offence, there is a risk that other people's words will be subjected to potentially controlling and divisive scrutiny: 'disabling' people for fear of using the 'wrong' words. Ironically, such controlling behaviour, when it comes to predetermining what language others are expected to use, can even be exerted unintentionally by otherwise well-meaning proponents of equality!

The essential issue to recognize is that words can mean different things to different people. In the case of this book, readers are respectfully encouraged to read the material whilst also appreciating the positive intentions of the writer – *not* just based on what terminology the reader prefers. If people use words that are then taken the wrong way, despite their best intentions, this is arguably disabling to the person using the words, and we get nowhere!

Needs and aspirations

We all know of people who do not like to be referred to as 'disabled'. We also know people who do not like to be described as having an 'impairment'. We might also have heard people questioning the attention or emphasis given to the word 'need' over other aspirational considerations. Before long we will have no words left.

For the purposes of writing this book, the preference is to underline that *we all have needs* – and there is no exception to this – so there is parity here! Even so, some have potentially greater needs than others. Without acknowledging this, we will not take the necessary steps to make life easier for those amongst us who face barriers that have not yet been addressed. However, whilst we refer to needs, let us not forget that we all generally have *aspirations* too.

Models of disability

Whilst aiming for a universal design approach in this book, when referring to disability, the convention followed here is close to the social model[1] of disability rather than the medical model. In the social model, disability is more defined by barriers in the environment than by medically identified impairments of the individual (Figure 1.1). 'Impairment' is therefore taken to refer to that aspect of someone's experience that is likely to lead a person to find certain activities more difficult than others to the extent that they are more likely to be disabled by barriers that have not been addressed by society. When referring to disabled people, therefore, I am generally referring to people within a cultural context of barriers that they experience.

Having referred to the social model of disability, it may also be helpful to introduce one further model, which could be described as the collaborative model or co-ability model. This is a model named as such by me but one that I have heard referred to in similar ways by others. In this model, the emphasis is not on attributing a cause to disability but about us all having a variety of abilities, needs and aspirations, so that each of us has the potential to bring something positive to the table and thereby remove barriers through collaboration, irrespective of our own difficulties (Figure 1.2). This model takes on a much more universal perspective of need.

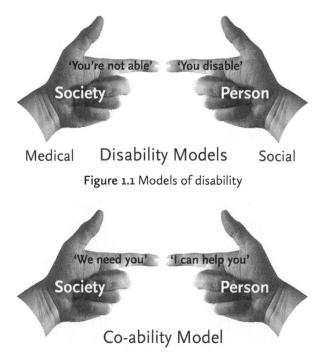

Figure 1.1 Models of disability

Figure 1.2 Collaborative or co-ability model

More often than not, this book will generally refer to 'neurological experience', as this covers everyone whilst also having the added poignancy of covering people who have more accentuated neurological experiences. Even so, it will sometimes be necessary to place an emphasis on a particular set of experiences by referring to underlying neurological impairments, difficulties and needs.

Some people prefer the term 'neurodiversity' or 'neurodivergence', but this is again open to interpretation. Philosophically, neurodiversity includes everyone, because we are all diverse! However, some will use the term neurodiversity to distinguish themselves from people with intellectual impairments and as a way of referring to neurological experiences such as autism, dyslexia, migraine and the like. Some may refer to certain minds as being either 'neuro-typical' or 'neuro-atypical', and some will object to these distinctions too.

Others will want to distinguish their specific experience of neurodiversity from having a mental illness or an intellectual learning difficulty. Whilst to some extent this is understandable, since not all neurological experiences are the same, this runs the risk of making people with an intellectual learning difficulty or a mental illness feel excluded and overlooks some commonality of experience.

Divisive use of language

I, as someone with personal experience of dyslexia, am therefore uncomfortable with the value judgments implied when some people overtly make a distinction between people with one form of impairment such as dyslexia and people with intellectual learning difficulties.

Sometimes a person perceives that when people say 'oh, dyslexics are intelligent' that in some way they are implying that dyslexics are more worthy of our attention than other people who have intellectual difficulties. Although the disparity between communication difficulties and intellectual difficulties is perhaps what has highlighted the presence of dyslexia (when there is no other apparent explanation for a person's difficulties), it also belies the fact that dyslexia does not necessarily mean that a person has a pronounced intellect! And if they did or did not have a pronounced intellect, should that make a difference to how others behave towards them?

Chosen terminology

This book therefore seeks to include everybody, and as such includes those with *any* accentuated neurological experience. This includes people with and without learning difficulties/intellectual impairments as well as people with or without mental health experiences. As a result, the preference in this book is to refer to people as having either 'neurological experience', 'neurological needs', 'neurological impairment' or 'neurological difficulties' – depending on the points that are to be put across. If, however, readers wish to substitute 'neurodiversity' for any of my preferred phrases, then I am quite happy if they do so – whilst holding on to an inclusive and universal interpretation.

Voice and invisibility

Perhaps one of the key issues to recognize is the relative invisibility of most neurological impairments. Sometimes, people with neurological impairments are not even seen as being disabled people because we/ they will not necessarily 'look disabled'. This invisibility also stems from people tending to be reluctant to talk about neurological issues because of the fears that some people have, even to the point that some disabled people with visible impairments are eager not to be perceived as having a neurological impairment. To some extent this is understandable, but it can make people with neurological impairments feel as though they are treated as an 'underclass' – even amongst some other disabled people.

The extent to which neurological difficulties can affect confidence, communication and social interactions tends to mean that there is also a lack of 'voice'. Consequently, the needs of people with neurological impairments are often neglected. Furthermore, the limited extent to which neurological impairments are perceived as a subject to talk about does not help matters either. This is despite the prevalence of neurological impairments and neurological episodes experienced within the population being arguably much greater than people realize.[2] This observation is not meant to diminish the significance of the experiences of disabled people with visible impairments but instead is meant to help redress perceptions. This book therefore seeks provide an amplified voice when thinking about our neurological needs within the context of commissioning and designing environments.

2

Learning from People on the Autistic Spectrum

...*and* with Other Neurological Experiences

Like a canary in a coal mine alerted miners in a bygone age, the neurological experiences of people with accentuated neurological experiences teach us to pay attention to the stressful aspects of environments around us – to the benefit of us all.

Autism[1]

It is quite apparent that of the accentuated neurological experiences that people can have, it is people's experience of autism that perhaps most strongly highlights the significance of the impact of environments on our neurological wellbeing. Rather like the canary in the coal mine analogy, the experiences of people on the autistic spectrum have the potential to alert everyone as to what they should pay attention to.

If we are to address the negative impacts that some environments can have on everyone's wellbeing, we need to listen to people on the autistic spectrum as well as others with accentuated neurological experiences. If we are to create new environments conducive for our neurological wellbeing, perhaps we also need to learn to recognize which environments enable us all to metaphorically 'sing a song of wellbeing'.

Universal experiences

Although it is stating the blatantly obvious, we need to acknowledge that without our senses we struggle to connect with the world around us! After all, it is our senses that alert us to the existence of various signals that we pick up from both spatial and social environments.

Apart from a relatively small contingent of architects, psychologists and neuroscientists, what seems not to have been so readily acknowledged within the practice of architecture and design is the impact that the design of environments has on our senses and therefore our minds. Even then (whilst this is an anecdotal observation gleaned from reading what some have written), it seems as though some of the architects who are interested in this area gravitate more to the esoteric end of the subject without much apparent practical understanding of diverse human factors. This results in a tendency to overlook people with more accentuated neurological experiences.

It is also apparent in the design of some specialist and even general health and care settings that there is a lack of awareness of the impact of poor social and spatial environments, such that some of the very healthcare environments in which people are being treated are actually making the situation worse for people with accentuated neurological needs![2]

Meanwhile, insights have been gained through observing the impact that sensory processing and integration difficulties has on how we all handle inputs from both the spatial and social environments around us. The work of psychologist and occupational therapist Dr Jean Ayres[3] did much to highlight this important subject, having sought to better understand the needs of children with sensory processing and integration difficulties – many of whom were on the autistic spectrum. Occupational therapist Dr Zoe Mailloux[4] also has particular interests in identifying sensory aware and friendly environments.

Furthermore, occupational therapist Dr Winnie Dunn[5] has written a book called *Living Sensationally: Understanding Your Senses*,[6] which expresses the universal significance that sensory processing and integration has for how we all differ from one another in our sensory profiles. We are all therefore on a sensory spectrum ranging from hypo- to hyper-sensitivity and passive to active responses to sensory stimuli from our environments. Perhaps we can all identify with times when we avoid certain sensory stimuli and other times when we seek sensory stimulus. The concept of different learning styles would further echo this kind of diversity when you realize that visual, auditory, kinaesthetic, multisensory, reflective, individual-working, group-working and other learning styles are all indicators of sensory processing and integration profiles and the strengths and so-called 'weaknesses' that we all have.

Childhood experiences

Even though it could be said that the experiences of children on the autistic spectrum most readily highlight the significance of our senses (and the attending processes and integration that our brains undertake), it is also quite apparent that the experiences of other children in general shed further light on the subject of designing environments with respect to our minds.

You could easily overlook the significance of changes in the brain as we develop and the differing needs for sensory stimulation that we have at different stages in life. Perhaps a key stage to recognize is that of childhood, as this is a stage when the brain has to learn and take on board new sensory experiences, process them, integrate them, make sense of them and act on them.

For example, children have to make sense of what they hear. Imagine you as a child are in a classroom with poor acoustics, where there is excessive background noise and the space is too reverberant. It is quite possible that in such circumstances you would not be able to hear the vowels in a teacher's speech.[7] Whilst most adults will usually have acquired the ability to fill in the blanks, a child will not necessarily have learnt to do this and will struggle in their learning as a result. Some children have a need to move and be active in order to learn, such that if there is insufficient opportunity to exercise their need for movement, or to learn by doing, they will struggle to learn.[8]

Likewise, some children learn visually and struggle if they have little access to visual stimuli. For example, it has been discovered that when parents are told that a child has been born with little vision, parents will tend to stop addressing the child's face anymore and the child will then lose the last bit of vision they have. However, if the parents are encouraged to continue addressing the child's face, continue normal behaviour and create a strong visual environment, the child has a better prospect of developing their visual abilities. This idea about parental behaviour is attributed to Professor François Vital-Durand, a French scientist, and he spoke about it at a conference on child vision in the '90s. The closest reference to this is found in a chapter in *Infant Vision* by Vital-Durand and his colleagues from the UK.[9]

Dementia[10]

Perhaps the other most significant source of learning is the experiences of people living with dementia. Whilst sensory processing and integration factors help shed some light on the experiences of people living with dementia, there are a variety of other significant and important observations that add further insight into the subject of designing environments with the mind in mind.

The importance of perception and of meaning given to what we sense becomes clearer when we listen to and observe the experiences of people living with dementia. For example, the significance of environmental context to memory becomes clearer, particularly when we look at memory's different forms, such as long-term, short-term, working, factual and emotional memory.[11] Consequently maintaining familiar environments and providing clear wayfinding are important design considerations.

Brain/nerve trauma/damage

Whilst it seems that awareness of the impact that environments can have on people on the autistic spectrum or living with dementia is more prevalent, it is also apparent that people with other brain-related experiences also shed similar light on the environment about us. People who have experienced strokes or brain injury, and to whom I have spoken, recount how certain environments pose a challenge to a similar degree as that recounted by people on the autistic spectrum. Brainline feature an article called 'Lost and Found: Dealing with Sensory Overload After Brain Injury', which provides insight into this experience.[12] Similarly, people with multiple sclerosis or Parkinson's to whom I have also spoken have highlighted neurological experiences relating to sensory processing and integration and not just physiological/mobility difficulties. This is also apparent in studies undertaken, such as those at the Karolinska Institute in Sweden.[13]

Physiological factors

If someone has a physiological impairment related to their sight and/or hearing, then this can have added neurological implications when operating in difficult spatial or social environments. This is because processing and integrating sensory information without one or more of a person's senses means that person has fewer senses with which their mind might then decipher the available spatial and/or social signals.

Despite this, some people, such as John Hull, experience the world positively with a perspective that others might not have.[14] However, without additional support, others with visual and/ or hearing impairments can become more isolated. Isolation and loneliness can then lead to psychological implications for individuals with sight and/or hearing impairments. Nevertheless, it must be stressed that just because someone has a sight and/or hearing impairment, it does not necessarily mean that they are isolated or have especially accentuated neurological experiences; it is that the potential risks are higher. Consequently, it is important for neurological reasons that visual and acoustic environments support the function of people's available senses, especially where people might want to meet others.

Anecdotal conversations that I have had with two people who had had ankle injuries also indicated that before their injuries healed, walking was made that much harder when subject to visual noise (i.e., pervasive and uncontrollable stimuli) in the form of repetitive or dazzling visual patterns. Arguably, such visual noise not only increases cognitive load but perhaps delays the flow of the deciphering and decoding of the environment that is necessary in order to walk without further injury.

Dyslexia and dyscalculia[15]

Some people with dyslexia, such as me, can recount how the auditory environment can have an impact on their thinking processes and deciphering what people are saying. Other people with dyslexia recount how black text on white backgrounds can be difficult to read and how different-coloured backgrounds help. These experiences further add to the significance of sensory environments.

People with dyscalculia tend to find arithmetic concepts too abstract and/or too difficult to remember. Other than where someone has another specific learning difficulty, it is not clear what the direct implications for design would be when considering dyscalculia, other than perhaps being careful to consider how time is displayed.

Dyspraxia[16]

Dyspraxia affects people's physical coordination within the world about them – where coordination of sensory inputs and outputs associated with body position (proprioception), balance (vestibular), touch (tactile) and vision are difficult. Consequently, uneven floor surfaces, complex visual environments and other complex interactions are likely to make navigation and coordination difficult for people with dyspraxia.

Learning difficulties[17]

People with learning difficulties, whilst having diverse needs and aspirations, can also shed light on how we might better design environments. If nothing else, it is the diversity of interests and abilities that people with learning difficulties will have that ought to persuade us to consider the *possible* and not limit our expectations as to what people can and cannot do.

Some learning difficulties are specific and are experienced by people with average or even particularly high intellectual abilities. These specific learning difficulties include dyslexia and dyscalculia. Nevertheless, many people with learning difficulties will also have intellectual difficulties. Even then, some (and yet *not all*) people with intellectual learning difficulties can have significant abilities to relate exceptionally well to other people or to undertake particular activities with focus and dedication.

Some people with learning difficulties may also have a variety of other multiple impairments, ranging from mild to profound – whether physical, sensory or neurological. Some folks with more profound and severe learning difficulties may also be on the autistic spectrum and provide us all with further insights as a result.

Perhaps the most important thing to remember is that interests, abilities and preferences will be diverse amongst people with intellectual or profound and multiple learning difficulties just like they are in society in general. For example, I have friends with intellectual learning difficulties who are a huge encouragement to me personally:

- One friend assists others with their public transport navigation needs.

- Another is an experienced actor.

- Another loves reading the Bible.

- Another is a 'philosopher' of sorts.

- Another cares deeply about others' wellbeing.

- Another has a smile to cheer.

- Another is passionate about truth.

- Another is really good at remembering people's names.

- Another speaks two languages.

- Another has a pioneering and leadership role in their local church community.

The most dedicated and patient man that I have ever known is a person with learning difficulties, who would wait patiently with focused attention whilst his friend (with a severe stutter) endeavoured to communicate.

All of these friends have significant learning difficulties, and yet they have more to their personalities than what society all too often assumes. Do we consider how we might design environments that welcome and include people with learning difficulties and offer them opportunities to get involved? What management, information and design considerations might make this easier?[18]

Migraines, epilepsy, phobias, etc.

According to the Migraine Trust, 1 in 7 people experience migraine,[19] and according to the Epilepsy Society, 1 in 50 people will have epilepsy at some time in their life and 1 in 20 will have a one-off seizure.[20] Of these people, some will be able to recount environmental triggers, not only triggers such as lighting but also patterns and other sensory stimuli. This field of work is something that Dr Alex Shepherd[21] is looking into. Professor Arnold Wilkins has also written a book called *Visual Stress*,[22] which describes the wider field of visual stress, including migraine and epilepsy. He has also explored the phenomenon of trypophobia, which is when people experience a sense of revulsion when they see a close pattern of holes (Figure 2.1).

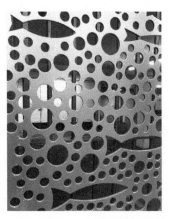

Figure 2.1 Design liable to induce trypophobia

Furthermore, people with severe shyness or with face blindness (where people find it difficult to recognize faces) have specific experiences related to their social and physical environment. It is important to consider how to incorporate different social opportunities and avoid people having to face social interactions that they are not prepared for.

It is worth remembering too that some people with neurological experiences such as severe vertigo (often induced by acrophobia) (Figure 2.2), claustrophobia (Figure 2.3) and agoraphobia (Figure 2.4) have a specific experience related to the spatial environment.

Figure 2.2 Acrophobia/vertigo-inducing view

Figure 2.3 Claustrophobia can influence how we respond to confined space
By Hannah Maslin

Figure 2.4 Agoraphobia can significantly impact how
we view the prospect of external environments
By Hannah Maslin

Consequently, designing environments that prevent people feeling
trapped is beneficial. For example, providing some toilets that are
spacious and externally lit may help some individuals who find small
spaces problematic. When designing window, floor, stair, bridge and
building edges, a visual means of providing reassurance may reduce
vertigo for some people. Similar issues arise when designing lifts
both for people with acrophobia and claustrophobia, depending
on how visually enclosed they are. Good signage can also alleviate

anxiety and allay fears of feeling trapped in complex or long and enclosed spaces. Michael Kindred has published an e-booklet called *Hidden Fear*,[23] which provides some useful insights into phobias and what design features can exacerbate phobias.

Mental illness

With 1 in 6 of us experiencing a mental health problem in any given week,[24] mental health needs impact on us all – if not directly, then through people we know. As with learning difficulties and other neurological experiences, the experiences of people with mental health difficulties/illness are broad and varied. Mental health illness can range from relatively mild and common episodes of anxiety/ neurosis to relatively uncommon, severe and lengthy periods of neurosis or psychosis.

Some confuse mental illness with learning difficulties and other neurological experiences. On occasion it is apparent that a person can have a neurological impairment and a mental illness – particularly where the needs associated with the impairment are not adequately met. Sometimes an illness is so significant it could be described as a long-term impairment, and that person may experience disability within society as a result.

Even without an in-depth exploration of sensory integration needs, it is apparent from empirical observation that the quality of both our physical and mental health is significantly impacted by the surrounding environment. On one hand we have sick building syndrome (a collection of eye, skin, nose, respiratory and fatigue symptoms, including headaches, thought to be triggered or made worse by the way some buildings are designed or the by materials found in them), and on the other hand we have reports that patients in hospitals with views of natural environments recover more quickly.[25] How much more might we better understand the causal links between physical health, mental health and environments?

Behavioural difficulties

It is often be assumed that neurological difficulties will be accompanied by behavioural difficulties. However, severe behavioural difficulties are relatively rare and should not automatically be associated with other neurological difficulties. Moreover, some of what we describe as 'behaviour' can be little more than stress responses to sensory overload or deprivation from either the spatial or social environments we find ourselves in. For example, Sensory Integration Education[26] has in its training material the statement 'if you see behaviour – think sensory'. By extension you could perhaps say:

'See behaviour – think environment.'

Consequently, it is especially important to understand what the environmental triggers are for behaviours, in order to either remove the cause of stress or better enable a person to manage their stress levels according to the options available within their environment – provided, that is, that there are options available in the first place. Essentially, exploring options for minimizing stress is one of the principal reasons for this book.

If we get design right, we could be providing opportunities for people to manage their stress well before their stress levels become so intense that their response is 'flight' or 'fight'. Even so, there are some individuals whose level of stress and whose need is so great, that some environments will require a greater level of design consideration. Otherwise, these environments run the risk of exacerbating stress and leaving some people more vulnerable in the circumstances. This is one of the subjects covered in Chapter 43, Safeguarding of Wellbeing.[27] This chapter also touches on the potential behavioural implications for those around an individual when someone experiences exceptionally high stress levels within an inadequate environment.

Medication/drugs

Whilst it is important not to confuse legitimate prescribed medication with drug abuse, it is nevertheless worth mentioning that both use of prescribed medication and drug abuse can have a significant impact on how our neurological processes work, depending on the active properties of the substance in question. In some scenarios, medication will help a person's neurological processes within an environment. In other scenarios, medication and especially drug abuse can give rise to short- or long-term side effects and/or difficulties. Either way, it is worth emphasizing that the environment is the context and that there is interplay between minds, environments and medication/drugs. We should not therefore ignore this relationship, particularly when it comes to designing environments where people are on medication or are receiving treatment for addiction.

In certain circumstances, it could be argued that the availability of more appropriately designed environments provides an opportunity to avoid the over-prescription of medication and to avoid their consequential side effects. This could especially be said in consideration of medication in response to behavioural difficulties. For example, significant behavioural improvements amongst people with dementia have been achieved through environmental improvements, reducing or removing the need for medication to manage behavioural difficulties.[28] In other circumstances, when seeking to help people who experience adverse side effects of medication or people who have abused drugs, it is worth considering the environmental factors that could make things either more manageable or more difficult.

Compound neurological experiences

As has already been stated, some people will have more than one impairment/experience/need. Just because a person has a less obvious impairment does not mean that they do not have other more obvious conditions or impairments as well. For example, people with Down's syndrome sometimes have associated heart problems and/or visual impairments as well.

People living with dementia can also experience accompanying effects of aging relating to mobility, vision and hearing. I also knew of a person with Down's syndrome and another person with Asperger's syndrome who both developed dementia. This goes to show that it is not good just to assume that experience gained from studying one 'diagnosis' will tell you how to design an environment. This is why:

> it is better to learn from a variety of experiences and let these diverse experiences inform an inclusive and universal approach to design.

Even where we are looking at specialist environments, only once we enable the establishment of a universally designed, mind-friendly environment should we then consider specific adjustments where people are known to have particular needs related to their diagnosis.

Family, friends and support workers

Whilst many disabled people, including people with neurological difficulties, are very independent, it is apparent that those around an individual can have a significant impact on that individual's wellbeing and vice versa. Those around an individual include family, friends and colleagues. Those within a person's support network (whether formal or informal) can all too easily find themselves in an inadequate environment and then experience neurological difficulties themselves as a result.

Support may simply be in an assistive and/or enabling role. Sometimes, where it is perceived that someone might be vulnerable, assistance and enabling roles can be accompanied by enhanced safeguarding responsibilities.[29] It is crucial, therefore, to understand that members of a particular person's support network also have their own neurological and psychological needs and that these can be significantly impacted if an environment is inadequate.

I have experience of working in a variety of specialist environments, including some very inadequate environments. Whilst this did not pose me direct personal difficulties, it did nevertheless provide me with insights as to the consequential implications that some environments could have on people and those within a person's support network. This in part has informed the writing of this book.

Learning from OT, Psychology, UX and Inclusive Design

There are particular hot spots of knowledge relevant to enabling mind-friendly environments.

Occupational therapy (OT)

The field that has most (but not exclusively) informed the writing of this book is the sensory integration specialism within occupational therapy. According to Sensory Integration Education,[1] sensory integration theory is the theory 'about how our brain receives and processes sensory information so that we can do the things we need to do in our everyday life'. Whilst general psychology knowledge and some specific disciplines within psychology have shed some light on the subject, for me, it is sensory integration theory within occupational therapy that has provided a better grasp of the significance of the sensory world when it comes to how our minds function within spatial and social environments. Much of the thinking on this subject was developed by Dr A. Jean Ayres[2] (who was an occupational therapist and psychologist) and others observing the experiences of people on the autistic spectrum and with other related neurological experiences. However, this knowledge, whilst relevant to designing environments, has remained mainly within the realm of therapeutic intervention. This book seeks to close the gap.

QUEEN MARGARET UNIVERSITY LRC

Psychology: scientific research

Several scientific research disciplines in psychology shed light on the subject of design and the environment. For example:

- Environmental psychologists[3] have looked at various aspects of the subject, including how people identify with place, how we develop personal space and how we interact in space.

- Occupational psychologists such as Dr Craig Knight[4] and researchers who study people within work environments have identified that control over one's working environment enhances productivity.

- Human factors psychology[5] has observed how people interact with the world around them and perceive things, their meanings and the metaphors that they develop for what they see and hear.

- Experimental psychologists and cognitive neuroscientists such as Dr Alex Shepherd[6] and Arnold Wilkins[7] have uncovered how some patterns can pose a visual challenge. For example, in 2018, Wilkins, Penacchio and Leonards published 'The Built Environment and Its Patterns: A View from the Vision Sciences',[8] which explains the relationship between visual patterns and human responses such as stress.

- It has also emerged under separate studies that as opposed to causing a problem, many (but not all) opportunities to view natural environments have the propensity to improve recovery from illness/hospitalization and to improve productivity at work.[9]

Service design[10]

Other disciplines that often apply psychology are UX design (user experience/usability design) and service design. Whilst these are most often applied to the design of customer journeys through services and how people navigate web and IT interfaces, they can also be applied to polices, products and the design of built environments too. This is because if you engage with the underlying philosophy of service design (that the end result of a design should be a service, attentive to a positive user experience) then it makes sense to consider how people engage with an environment on a neurological level. Indeed, it seems strange that many embark on the design of environments without carefully considering the diverse users and their diverse experiences of the services offered within these environments.

User testing surveys are common to UX and service design practices, as is the creation of persona narratives. Persona narratives are where a handful of fictional user stories are developed, much like creating the cast of a film, so that those involved in a project can readily bring to mind the range of people using the environment. This can be particularly effective if diversity has been built into the stories from the beginning. Consequently, both UX surveys and persona narratives can be immensely powerful means of engaging with people's needs, especially if the neurological dimension of end users is considered.

Inclusive design and access consultancy[11]

The primary field of application for this book is inclusive design and access consultancy as applied to architecture and other design disciplines within the built environment. Many access consultants prefer to use terms like 'inclusive design' and 'universal design' over the term 'access', based on the belief that design is about considering everyone in an integrated way and not just about 'special' provision. Crucial to inclusive design consultancy is stakeholder engagement where possible and an understanding of the management dynamic in delivering an inclusive user experience. Properly understood, this realm of expertise can also be perceived as a form of service design consultancy, as it is able to shed light on the likely user experience of people within an environment.

4

Design as Social Prescribing

This chapter equates appropriate inclusive design intervention (that engages with people's neurological needs) to social prescribing.

Many doctors recognize the value of prescribing courses of action other than medicine (such as therapy, counselling, walking, exercise or cookery classes). Similarly, it could be argued that there is a need to see the importance of commissioners 'prescribing' better physical and sensory environments.

The irony is that whilst therapy and tutorial interventions are all very well and good, people may have to function in environments that are not conducive to their wellbeing. How much better would healthcare thinking be if we also considered the design of context, such as the environments in which people lived and worked? Okay, home environments may be easier for people to adapt to their needs, but what about work environments?

Indeed, several sources and conversations that I have had indicate that some particular healthcare settings themselves give rise to the very sensory stresses that some people (especially babies or people with accentuated neurological needs) struggle to cope with.[1] Consider hospital wards that you have visited and remember the hard surfaces, noise and intense lighting and how you would consider yourself fortunate if you were able to look out at nature? Think also of the deep floor plans and the propensity for many hospital facilities to have no views out at all. Then think of how difficult it often is to navigate around old and sprawling hospitals such as Bristol Royal Infirmary and how disorientating they can be!

In the workplace

In the past, it was much easier for office workers to personalize their workspaces. However, with the onset of open-plan offices, hot-desking and mandatory clear-desk policies, it has become a lot harder for people to adapt workspaces to their needs and aspirations. According to Dr Craig Knight, this is counterproductive and will affect output.[2]

In education

Other than healthcare and workplace environments, it is perhaps education environments that offer the greatest opportunities to bring the benefits of better 'mind-friendly' thinking. For example, one of the reasons for the UK Government's Building Bulletin 93[3] on acoustics in schools being brought out was the recognition that poor acoustics in schools meant that not only did children struggle to hear but they also struggled to decipher what was being said, pay attention, concentrate and therefore think and learn. Problems included poor reverberation times within classrooms, noise from neighbouring spaces and noise from outdoors, especially where classrooms faced onto busy roads.

In retail

Perhaps some people would get out and about out more, benefit from greater levels of social interaction and exercise more if the design of retail, visitor and leisure facilities more fully considered diverse physical and neurological needs.

Some might think from what we experience of some retail, visitor and leisure environments that such environments are not fully appreciating the benefit of mind-friendly environments. Perhaps businesses are losing out on customers that are put off

by the sensory implications of the environments that they are
in. Apparently, IKEA stores are designed the way they are – with
long prescribed routes past all their products – to increase sales.[4]
But how many people are put off by the lack of rest points, by
how protracted and disorientating the routes are and the lack of
connection with outdoors?

In custody

Judicial/custodial environments, especially old Victorian prisons
such as Pentonville Prison in London, are arguably amongst the
most profoundly troubling environments given that prisons are
often designed with little attention to their neurological impact and
that a large percentage of prisoners have accentuated neurological
needs.[5] For example, poor natural and artificial lighting, poor
acoustics and lack of access to nature are likely to make situations
much more stressful for some prisoners, especially those with
underlying neurological and sensory processing difficulties.

5

Prescription to Commissioning

This chapter conveys what needs to be done in order to transfer and implement knowledge between the different worlds of prescribing and commissioning.

How comfortable are members of the therapeutic, medical, teaching and social services disciplines with expressing themselves in a commissioning mode rather than a prescribing mode? It seems that if we are to see environments change for the better, then people-facing disciplines need to be able to find the voice to express themselves during the commissioning of new or refurbished environments. However, it is all too easy for therapists and others who are familiar with aspects of sensory integration theory and other models for therapeutic intervention to find that they are unable to express themselves in a design commissioning context, especially when others are assuming the commissioning role. Commissioners may seek your input; however, you might struggle to frame your perspective in a way that you feel they will understand. Conversely, they may fail to involve you sufficiently from the outset. Consequently, it is important to:

- recognize the potential of having an influence on the context in which your 'clients' find themselves[1]

- find a voice[2]

- not be put off by those more familiar with design commissioning[3]

- understand the benefit of seeking allies and those able to bridge between the two worlds within a project[4]

- understand the need for a strategy[5]

- recognize the benefit of the right experts[6]

- understand language and methodologies[7]

- be proportionate in what you ask for.[8]

Intervention in context

When members of the therapeutic, medical, teaching and social services communities carry out their daily interventions, assisting others within their respective areas, it will become apparent that despite the focus of one's own discipline, there are other issues limiting what can be achieved within a single discipline. However, everyone's lives (and the various disciplines that have emerged to help) are played out in context. In other words, all environments have operational implications for human activity, including the neurological processes that enable us to undertake these human activities. The potential offered by working together in a systematic way and seeking to address the contextual issues that clients/patients/students/employees face is significant. After all, what is a person likely to achieve if they fail to address the contextual issues amidst which people's minds struggle to function?

Finding a voice

Yes, you may not be a built-environment professional or designer, but design is about problem-solving, and everyone is a user of environments. Within your own discipline you will utilize problem-solving to some extent. Therefore, whilst you may not be sufficiently experienced and competent in designing built environments alone, a particularly good argument can be made for being involved in a co-production.[9] The key argument is that the construction phase of most built-environment projects represents a relatively small part of any whole-life costing for an environment. Indeed, so small are the constructional costs of a project in comparison with the operational costs of an organization (of which 'human resources' form a significant part), Paul Morrell, former chief construction advisor to the UK Government, has stated that construction costs can be effectively paid for by savings in operational costs brought about as a result of better design![10]

Finding confidence

The problem is that many people lack the confidence to hold their own amidst built-environment professionals. Whilst some built-environment professionals are eager to take on board operational considerations, others can portray arrogance as to their own expertise! This is usually because they lack confidence outside their own comfort zone and, like all of us, have limited expertise themselves. Most construction projects require several different disciplines to work together, and there is no rational reason why those who work with people within environments should be excluded from that process.

Seeking allies

Finding a voice and the necessary confidence on your own can often be difficult. Consequently, it is always worth finding allies.

- **Access consultants** with the necessary understanding of people's neurological needs would be the most natural external allies. However, you need internal allies within your organization in order to have the opportunity to get input from an access consultant. Some architects will also be good external allies, especially if they are keen to listen to and engage with the expertise of an access consultant with the appropriate knowledge of people's neurological needs.

- **Human resource managers, service managers and equalities officers** should ideally be amongst your most immediate allies. However, they may also face the same challenges as you do and feel one step removed from decisions about the environments that they find themselves in. Even so, there is benefit in numbers – and so it always worth getting these people on board, especially if you communicate in their respective professional 'languages'.

- **Facilities managers** – most organizations with responsibilities for property will have one or more people in a facilities management role. Depending on the organization, the role of overseeing facilities managers usually belongs to the chief operations officer (COO). Facilities management responsibilities, however, vary from one facilities manager to another. Some are contracted in and are focused on cleaning, maintenance, energy, security and cost savings – and less on what they might consider to be the 'finer' points of service. However, some facilities managers are those who not only have built-environment knowledge but also are engaged with what is going on at a human level.

To engage allies at a senior level, you will want to have assembled your evidence and put together the 'business case' with the help of your internal and external allies. The senior ally you really want to get the attention of is the person with the purse strings, such as someone in the chief financial officer (CFO) role. Again, you will need to have assembled your evidence. Despite your efforts, though, and even when you have put together a good case, you can all too easily find it difficult to persuade some decision-makers. Consequently, there are two further sets of allies:

- **Stakeholders:** such as employees, service users and customers, as these are the primary end users.

- **Family:** those in your organization who have direct family experience.

If your decision-makers have personal or family experience, then this can make a huge difference. There is a significant likelihood of there being some direct or indirect experience of accentuated neurological needs within most families, and people develop greater empathy if they are asked to reflect on this. Where there is empathy for the subject, you can often find that doors are easier to open. Consequently, it is worth getting to know the people who you want to be your key allies and discovering more about them and their families. Share your interests in an appropriate way and see whether they open up. If they do, you can then relate their experiences to what you are trying to do.

Strategy

Persuading COOs, CFOs or other senior directors usually involves getting a social return on investment (SROI) analysis done as it applies to what you are doing and helps you to find other benefits, risks and legal reasons to persuade your senior colleagues. This book should assist you with identifying the contributory factors for building an SROI case as well as addressing duties under legislation such as the Equality Act in the UK and equivalent legislation elsewhere.

The good news, however, is that if implemented as part of a new build project or within existing maintenance and refurbishment programmes, then much of the cost of implementing a mind-friendly design is likely to be neutral, negligible or moderate within the grand scheme of projects. Moreover, the benefits as they apply to in-use value are likely to pay for such costs, if any. However, even negligible or moderate costs can attract attention, unless there is a significantly robust defence, when built-environment professionals engage in so called 'value engineering' (VE).

Value engineering is a much-misappropriated term, as it usually degenerates into little more than cost cutting at the expense of value, unless, that is, people like you are prepared for the 'attack' on what you recognize as valuable and devise a defence strategy! Easy targets for VE will be lighting, landscape and other seemingly soft targets, which could have otherwise had a significant benefit for people's neurological wellbeing (if indeed they are implemented well in the design).

In order to build a defence to cost cutting, you still need to build not only the arguments for your case but also use your stakeholder capital in what you are doing. There is huge benefit to be had, therefore, from involving employees, service users and customers. Indeed, these people are essential allies. It is much harder for disinterested decision-makers to dismiss value-based arguments if they have to explain themselves to lots of stakeholders.

Utilizing expertise

Many a project would reap significant benefits were the needs of people within the built environment considered in depth, whether these needs be neurological or physiological. However, it is essential to understand the expertise gap that exists between the necessary people-facing skills and the necessary technical skills. When those from either skill set seek to address issues alone, they tend to either miss things or lose proportionality.[11] For this reason, it is judicious to insist on the input of an appropriately experienced access consultant[12] able to advise on inclusive design with the necessary bridging skill set. It is also essential to provide your backing to the access consultant, as voices internal to an organization are often needed in order to echo the external voice of the access consultant. Moreover, an access consultant is but one expert around any table, and they alone will not make the difference. Everyone needs to raise the human-centric design agenda and contribute their own expertise – with the help of the access consultant.

Project briefs

It is always worth familiarizing yourself with the language and methodologies of those you are seeking to influence. Within the realm of architecture and design, one of the key terms that you will need to be aware is 'brief development'. Simply put, good design does not just emerge out of thin air. If it does, you will be leaving too much to the architect's/designer's unbridled imagination!

A project brief is therefore necessary if architects and other built-environment professionals are to know what is expected of them. A brief is essentially a record of the commissioning organization's instructions to their design team. However, it is all too easy for project briefs to be so rigid that they inhibit designers from asking the right questions or do not provide sufficient information to set out expectations around human-centred design. This is why a brief-development process is so important and should not be left just to project managers. It is a process in which your voice needs to be heard alongside the access consultant who you have asked for. Ideally, the brief-development process should begin before the brief itself is written and continue after a design team has been taken on board.

To further the likelihood that the brief development and design process will take on board human-centred design considerations, it is worth drawing the project and design team's attention to service design methodology.[13] Unfortunately, many architects are not taught service design methodologies. Hence, it is worth introducing them as the basis by which you would like to see brief development undertaken.

Proportionality

When seeking proportionality in provision, you are seeking not to cut back on what you ask for but instead to make sure that you do not overstress one design idea over another. We are all individuals. This is equally the case amongst people on the autistic spectrum or with other diverse neurological experiences. Indeed, Stephen M. Shore said 'If you meet one person with autism, you've met one person with autism.'[14]

There are well-meaning theories out there that are based on some understanding of the issues but are at risk of over-prescribing one course of action. Just as with therapy and medical interventions, there is always a risk of an overdose based on a pet theory, and no less so when it comes to designing the built environment. It is rare that any environment is designed around one person. The risk is that a designer knows someone who has hyper-sensitivity to one thing and thinks that particular thing sets the tone for everything, when another person might have hypo-sensitivity to that same thing and need stimulus. So, whilst it is advisable to commission calm environments, you should avoid a 'one size fits all approach'. It is better to commission environments that provide choice and a degree of variety whilst getting the basics right in terms of reducing sensory stress.

6

For Whom or With Whom?

It is all too easy to see design as something that you do for people rather than with people.

As with the social and collaborative models of disability, needs and aspiration,1 a difference in attitude is necessary when embarking on inclusive and universal people-centric design. Sadly, attitudes have not moved much further on in this regard within architecture, interior design and landscape architecture. However, there are emerging design practices that are worth bearing in mind. They are summed up by the words engagement, co-production and service design. Such practices are quite simply about involving people and evaluating design with diversity in mind.

Engagement, co-production and service design

The philosophy behind service design is that anything a person designs, whether a policy, service, product or environment has a service function; otherwise, the design will have little or no real value in and of itself. The recipients of a service are diverse, and so giving attention to people's diverse needs and aspirations is critical. Hence, the associated methodologies to service design are engagement, co-production and the development of persona narratives.

- Stakeholder engagement is the bedrock of service design. The best stakeholder engagement is well prepared, informed and proportionate, where key stakeholders contribute, especially those with specific duties or with particularly valuable knowledge and/or experience.

- Co-production is where the designer takes on the role of facilitator and not 'dictator' of design and where key people are involved in the co-production of the design.

- Persona narratives are where the co-production project team write narratives for up to five or so fictional people who represent a diverse spread of need, aspiration and role. Persona narratives usually include both service recipients and service providers in the environment that is being designed. In lieu of any accompanying third-party stakeholder engagement, these personas can then become the means of testing out the design in between wider stakeholder engagement sessions. They help everyone consider how the design might function at a service level.

Whilst persona narratives remain fictional, they can be written in such a way as to draw upon real life examples that are known to the team, such as third-party stakeholders, colleagues, friends or even family members whom you would wish to be included. This approach then forms a useful means of undertaking the development of a project brief.[2]

It does not help stakeholder engagement if you go in totally cold without some sense of possible direction. What helps invigorate stakeholder engagement is the of use maps, plans, locational photographs, subject-related images and a series of apparently unrelated images that might be used to communicate ideas. Enthusiastic stakeholders can encourage people to share ideas – for example by writing down quick suggestions on sticky notes and using LEGO® bricks – and use different means of modelling ideas and concepts. You can also use online resources to facilitate the engagement process. For example:

- Confers[3] is an online, pay-to-use tool that provides the opportunity to use visual imagery and reach a specific, dispersed or wide audience.

- Service Design Tools, Service Design Toolkit and Q offer a range of free-to-use resources within group settings.[4]

Inclusive engagement[5]

When it comes to engaging people with accentuated neurological needs, it is important to try to be as inclusive and engaged as possible. Some of the issues that might be considered when consulting known individuals and planning for scenarios are as follows:

- Some, but not all, people with more accentuated neurological impairments may find aspects of communication difficult. This can be as a result of one or more factors and varies from person to person.

- Communication failure can be just as much a result of a failure of others to consult people with neurological impairments rather than as a result of an individual's neurological impairment.

- Although comprehension difficulties can be a significant factor for some people with neurological impairments, it should *not* be assumed that everyone with either neurological difficulties or communication difficulties will have comprehension difficulties.

- The rate at which spoken or written information can be decoded, or the rate at which information can be encoded into spoken or written form, can significantly influence communication. For example, it is thought that Einstein had either Asperger's syndrome or dyslexia (or even both) and that he would need time to decipher what others were saying to him.

- Interpretive and social difficulties can also present a challenge during the communication process for some people. For example, some people with autism/Asperger's syndrome can find 'reading' social signals or understanding subjective information difficult and may interpret information on a very objective and literal basis that was not intended. For this reason, it is important that you seek to ascertain whether someone has understood the information as you intended that information to be understood.

- Some people with neurological impairments can have emotional difficulties, which hinder their communication. For example, I once worked with an individual with learning difficulties whose emotional difficulties initially hid their capabilities.

- Some people with neurological impairment may not be that easy to understand. This can be because they are not able to speak clearly or at all.

- People familiar with an individual's needs tend to make sense of what is being said and may be available to assist with communication. What is being said can often make perfect sense when you know enough about the individual and how they understand the world about them.

- As with braille or BSL users, some people with learning difficulties will use other modes of communication, such as symbols and signing, to support their communication. A common system using symbols and signing is Makaton. The Makaton Charity[6] trains interpreters and translators to assist in dialogue with Makaton users and to prepare material for communication purposes.

- Some people with neurological impairments have multiple impairments. For example, it is not unusual for someone with Down's syndrome to have a visual impairment or hearing impairment, and some people will use BSL when their hearing impairment is more significant than their comprehension difficulties. Some people will need signing in the form of direct hand-to-hand touch signing, owing to having both a visual and hearing impairment.

- People charged with the task of consulting individuals with neurological impairment might find the prospect presents them with anxiety, especially if they find themselves interacting with someone whose form or expression or behaviour strikes them as being difficult to engage with. This is not the fault of the person with neurological impairment nor, for that matter, the listener. It may be that the listener needs to be honest about this anxiety and seek support when carrying out their task of consultation.

Avoid 'fluffy' engagement

Whilst 'ice breaking' and team-building exercises are good to begin with, what both participants in engagement and decision-makers really want to see progress. Design team members will also want to start identifying outcomes that give them greater clarity as to what is required of them through developing the brief.

There is therefore a reputational risk for organizations commissioning engagement and for engagement practices itself, when so-called engagement is either poorly structured, is undertaken as an 'end unto itself' or is used as a smoke screen to inform stakeholders of decisions already taken. This is because information masquerading as engagement and consultation runs the risk of losing credibility with stakeholders, and poorly structured 'fluffy' engagement activities tend to antagonize participants if they do not start to establish meaningful and timely outcomes. What is more, whilst certain engagement techniques may be good in principle, the true measure of success is the emergence well-reasoned human-centred design as a result of including those with relevant human-centred design knowledge alongside building users.

The Human Experience

In this section we will discover the common human experience in which we all (to varying degrees) find aspects of environments around us neurologically beneficial or problematic.

We know that some people have a particular neurological make-up that makes processing signals from social, sensory and other neurological processes especially difficult. Experts, including Dr A. Jean Ayres,[1] started exploring this subject in the 1900s – mainly within a therapeutic context. Organizations such as Sensory Integration Education[2] and The National Autistic Society[3] are now disseminating that information. As a consequence, we know that environments, and the social, sensory and neurological processes that go on within them, can have a significant impact on how people function. From this research, what could we learn and apply to the benefit of everyone?

7

Diversity

Whilst there is much that all humans have in common, a firm grasp on the relevance of diversity makes for better understanding of what works best.

From the perspective of the client or designer, one of the key questions when considering new – and re-considering existing – buildings, interiors, urban realms and landscapes, is: For whom are we commissioning or designing? If you look at the history of design in the West, it is apparent that much of it has been dominated by a male, white, Western, middle-class, non-disabled and neuro-typical view of the world!

Whilst it debatable whether someone with quite as exceptional abilities as Leonardo Da Vinci can be described as neuro-typical, it is apparent that his *Vitruvian Man*[1] (Figure 7.1) gave us a particular image of whom we were supposedly designing for. Similarly, Le Corbusier's *Modulor Man*[2] (Figure 7.2) did much the same to limit the perception of humanity's diversity in the mind of modern designers.

Moreover, it seems that Western cultures (such as those influenced by Greek thinking) have often described objects in a non-functional way and in a way that loses sight of what something is for; whereas other cultures – such as the ancient Hebrew culture – described things on the basis of what they were for. Consequently, it has been all too easy for designers to abstract and over-simplify their thinking from the purpose of their design and from whom they are designing for.

Furthermore, 'seeing is believing' is an all-too-common statement within today's materialistic cultures, such that when it comes to understanding the neurological realm, many people have found it easy to ignore the reality of what they cannot see. However, switching this mantra round to 'believing is seeing' opens up the possibility of not only grasping some profound truths behind the world around us but also taking into consideration people's account of their unseen neurological experiences.

Figure 7.1 Vitruvian Woman caricature of *Vitruvian Man*

Figure 7.2 Modulor Woman caricature of *Modulor Man*

Envelope of need

Even when it comes to people's physiological needs, let alone people's neurological needs, designers have too often neglected designing in a sufficiently diverse and human-centric way. However, if you were designing an aircraft, you would design it to a 'performance envelope'. Outside of that envelope, the aircraft is unlikely to function properly. Within that envelope, however, it would be expected to function. Consequently, if we consider diverse needs and more accentuated atypical neurological experiences, we are much more likely to come up with an envelope of performance for our design that works for far more people. This is described by the Clinton-Maslin Envelope of Need developed by me and one of my directors at the Schumacher Institute, Michael Clinton.[3] Designing with an envelope of need in mind, you are much more likely to arrive at more socially sustainable results and what we call universal and inclusive design. The Clinton-Maslin Envelope of Need embraces not only:

- neurological needs

but also:

- mobility

- vision

- hearing

- metabolic needs (see Figure 7.3)

whilst seeking to address the design implications of:

- logistics: people's personal logistics/journey

- legibility: the environment's legibility

- clarity: auditory and visual clarity of spaces

- psychology: neurological implications of the environment and

- ergonomics: the implications of how people interact with details and layout (see Figure 7.4).

Figure 7.3 Aide-mémoire for the envelope of need

Figure 7.4 Aide-mémoire for the envelope of design

Whilst much valuable work on design thinking has been based on observing people with particular neurological diagnoses such as autism and dementia, the need now is to learn from the experiences of people with a range of diagnoses to arrive at common approach to designing better environments for everyone, providing choice and opportunity for people with different needs.

8

Stress

This chapter focuses on learning about environments by identifying stress as one of the indicators that something is wrong.

Stress is something that we can all identify with. Much like pain, its symptoms are usually an indicator of something not being right. However, how often do we properly stop to consider the causes of our own stress and that of other people's? Where were we (or they) at the time? Did where we were have anything to do with causing us stress or increasing or decreasing pre-existent stress?

Stress as indicator

As we can see from the section 'Contextual Experience',[1] the situations we find ourselves in can have a significant bearing on how our minds function. Stress can then be an indicator of factors derived from, or made worse by, the environment – compounding any other stresses that we are experiencing.

We know from the experiences of those on the autistic spectrum, as researched by Dr A. Jean Ayres (mentioned earlier) and others, that environmental causes of stress can be amplified by how an individual processes sensory signals to the extent that certain frequencies of sound, pattern or light output can cause significant problems (see Figure 8.1). If our perception and interpretation of the world about us is in some way impaired through learning difficulties, mental illness or dementia, then you can also see how confusing and difficult-to-interpret environments (with poorly designed spaces, visuals, acoustics and wayfinding) can then give rise to even greater stress. For example, questions that may arise from such poorly designed environments might include:

- 'Is that an entrance I see?'

- 'Is that an even floor I see?'

- 'What did that person say?'

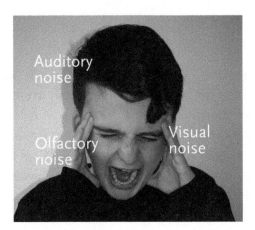

Figure 8.1 Stress can indicate contextual causes

Indicators of stress

How do we notice stress? Sometimes there are physiological responses to stress such as increased heart rate, breathing and perspiration. However, these are not always obvious to those around us. It is usually the perceived changes in behaviour that are the giveaways of stress. Even so, behaviour triggered by environmental stressors will not always be understood as a signal of underlying stress if the person observing them is not sensitive to such stressors. In such situations, without another's appreciation of the underlying causes, a person's behaviour might seem completely out of context and perceived as odd, rude or even aggressive.

If someone is subjected to pain, then there will usually be an aversive or defensive reflex action. Similarly, stress-related behaviours could be seen as an aversive or defensive reflex response to circumstances. All circumstances have a context, namely the sensory environment – both physical and social.

In Sensory Integration Education circles, there is a slogan in their training material that says 'See behaviour – think sensory.'[2] You might go further than this and say:

- 'see behaviour', then...

- 'think stress', then...

- 'think sensory', then...

- 'think environmental signals', then...

- 'think context', and then...

- 'think social/spatial configuration'.

Whilst the causes of stress are many and varied, the simple fact is that the environmental context can have a huge impact on how stress is either caused, amplified or diminished. This raises the question as to whether good design could go a long way to reducing stress and maybe therefore act as an alternative to more drastic interventions such as medication.[3]

9

Sensory Processing

This chapter introduces the subject of sensory processing and identifies how it connects our minds with environments around us.

Mind: brain with senses

We have already identified that our minds struggle to function without our senses being able to send us signals[1] or without our brain being able to cope with the sensory stimuli we receive.[2] However, it is not as if our sensory organs do all the work and achieve their ultimate purposes *without* neurological processes being involved. Vision is a classic example of how much of what we see – or perhaps more accurately 'perceive' – is reliant on our brains.

What we perceive with our eyes is reliant on our brain filling in and filtering significant amounts of information. To start with, it rotates the vision through 180 degrees since what is detected on the back of our eyes is upside down to begin with. Second, most of us have functioning colour receptors in our central vision with few in our peripheral vision, and it is our neurological processes that finish the 'rendering' of the peripheral image in our brain with colour information. However, if our brains were to fully process every bit of data that our eyes detect, then we would experience sensory overload (which is one of the things that many people on the autistic spectrum can experience). In order that we do not experience this sensory overload, our brain usually filters out much of the visual data that comes through our eyes. However, it will struggle in certain circumstances, such as when we are tired, are intoxicated, have some underlying impairment or are subjected to 'noisy' forms of visual signals to start with. We will explore what might constitute 'noisy' later.[3]

Similar processing complexities can also occur with our other senses. As I have already explained in the Preface, I found it difficult deciphering what people were saying to me when I was younger (and still do on occasions) and now realize that I find it particularly difficult to filter out certain sounds. Other people will have comparative difficulties with other senses such as touch, smell and taste. These experiences all go to show that sensory processing and integration is not a straightforward process. However, these sensory experiences all begin with inputs, and these inputs come from the physical and social environment around us.

Not only is sensory information being processed by our brains, but it is being brought together and integrated so that we make sense of the world around us and function within it. Take walking for example – it necessitates us deciphering the world around us through bringing together a variety of senses. These senses (where we have them in functioning order) include vision, a sense of balance and body position and the sensation of touch (as our feet come in contact with the surface we are walking across). In order to walk, our brain undertakes a significant amount of integrating the information from these different senses.

We will explore the design implications of sensory processing and integration under Section C[4] and Section E.[5] However, we will first take the opportunity here to set out a few paragraphs explaining what sensory processing and integration is and how it came to be understood.

Our senses

First, sensory processing and integration relates to a variety of senses, where sensory data is processed into intelligible information by our neurological processes. This sensory data involves the five senses that people are most aware of. These are:

- visual – i.e., sight via our eyes

- auditory – i.e., hearing via our ears

- olfactory – i.e., aroma via our nose

- gustatory – i.e., taste via our tongue's taste buds

- tactile – i.e., touch via our nerve endings, processed into sensations of deep pressure, discernible textures and/or pain.

However, there are more senses than these five alone. Three senses in particular have significance in the realm of physio therapy, occupational therapy and sensory integration therapy.[6] These are:

- vestibular – i.e., balance via our inner ears, processed into discernible vertical and horizontal orientation by our neurological processes

- proprioception – i.e., a sense of body position awareness, processed into discernible body positioning by our neurological processes

- interoception – i.e., a sense of internal body awareness, processed into discernible indicators by our neurological processes, as to what our internal systems (coronary, breathing, digestive, etc.) are telling us about their performance and any stress that we might be experiencing.

I would suggest, however, that there are yet further senses that are equally important when it comes designing environments (see Figure 9.1):

- thermal – i.e., a sense of temperature, processed by our nerves and neurological processes into discernible sensations of being either cold, warm or hot

- chronometric – i.e., sequential progression of changing light via our eyes, processed into a discernible sense of time between events.

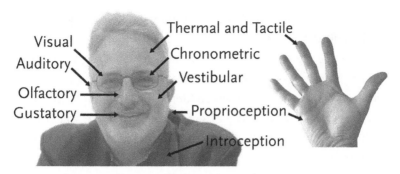

Figure 9.1 There are several senses

The significance of the latter two to the design of environments is that temperature is something that we take particular account of when we design buildings, and time is something that relates to memory, recollection of place and how people navigate through environments. Seen from a human perspective, however, temperature regulation is something that some can find difficult, not knowing whether they are hot or cold, or being particularly susceptible to feeling draughts. Finding a room too hot, too cold or draughty makes us feel uncomfortable and tired and can affect our ability to concentrate. Likewise, when it comes to the sense of time, some people with attention difficulties, Parkinson's disease or with the onset of dementia can find that they lose their sense of timing or orientation in time.[7]

Theoretical basis

Many of the initial observations with regard to sensory processing and integration and its complexities have arisen from those undertaking research and those working with children on the autistic spectrum and other neurologically diverse experiences. A pioneer in understanding this subject was Dr A. Jean Ayres, an American academic, psychologist and occupational therapist.[8] She developed what has become known as sensory integration therapy. She said that 'sensations are "food" or nourishment for the nervous system; the brain needs continuous variety of sensory nourishment to develop and then function'.[9] People likes Ayres recognized that some people find aspects of sensory processing and integration more difficult than others. Moreover, a substantial amount of scientific evidence shows that this process is not straightforward. Ayres' work provides clear evidence that it is possible with some therapeutic intervention to help children to both learn to process and integrate sensations more effectively and to make adjustments to their environment so that they are able to progress despite their difficulties.

Universal application

Have you ever wondered why some people fidget or draw doodles? You might be tempted to think that this is because people are not focusing on their work or paying attention to what they are being taught. However, fidgeting or doodling may be a person's strategy to maintain focus and pay attention or to help them think through the issues. We should remember, after all, that alongside learning to manage and cope with what our senses detect, our minds can also find it difficult to function without any sensory stimulation.[10]

Some of us will stimulate our thought processes through listening to music, sitting with a cup of coffee or looking out of the window. Positive emotional thought can also be at its strongest when snug furniture replicates the sensation of being held with a degree of deep pressure as if being hugged and held by loving parents. For some of us, our clearest thought processes occur when we are walking. You may observe that some people put their hands to their lips when thinking and considering what they might say. This is quite possibly an example of us stimulating the proprioceptive aspects of speech through the proprioceptive and tactile activity of our hands.

Unfortunately, apart from a few notable exceptions, some people think that sensory processing and integration is only really an issue for people with autism, rather than something that is capable of providing us with additional insights into the experience of diverse populations as a whole. As a consequence, it is assumed that sensory processing and integration should be considered only for specialist environments. Few consider the possibility that insights could be applied to environments as a whole. Dr Winnie Dunn's book, *Living Sensationally: Understanding Your Senses*,[11] does much to bring about a more universal understanding of the subject.

It is also worth recognizing that as we progress through life, our sensory processing capabilities change. When we are younger and brain plasticity is at its greatest, we are learning to process and integrate our senses. In other words, when we are born, we do not immediately make sense of the world around us. For example, when babies first begin to wave their hands in front of them, they are not only establishing a connection between sensory and motor input, but they are also learning to process and integrate their proprioceptive sense in conjunction with their visual sense.

What is also worth observing is the comparison between children and older adults when it comes to how they exercise their senses and how they react to sensory stimuli. If you observe children, they will tend to be doing all they can to exercise their sensory processing and integration activities – generating a lot of movement and noise whilst doing so. However, if you observe the reaction of some older adults to the sensory challenges posed by noisy, hyperactive children, you might detect a degree of sensory processing discomfort being experienced by the adults. Even so, you will also find some children – and not necessarily only those on the autistic spectrum – who recoil from some of the intense noise and movement exhibited by their peers.

Application within environments

Even though nowadays a few more people have a more universal understanding of sensory processing and integration, it still seems that more needs to be done to bridge the gap with the world of design. However, American academic and occupational therapist Dr Zoe Mailloux[12] (who worked with Dr A. Jean Ayres) has a particular interest in addressing sensory processing and integration challenges at source. For example, sensory integration specialists like Mailloux believe vestibular, proprioceptive and tactile senses have a regulatory effect on our sensory and neurological processes. Mailloux has consequently collaborated with Virco, a school chair manufacturer, to identify the benefits of providing school chairs[13] that rock and allow children to 'feed' their vestibular and proprioception senses whilst learning (Figure 9.2). This is just one example of how understanding our sensory and neurological processes should influence the commissioning and design of environments. We will explore this more in Section C.[14]

Figure 9.2 School chairs designed to rock
Image provided by Virco

10

Emotion, Meaning and Metaphor

This chapter takes a look at identifying the metaphorical, interpretative and emotional overlay that can arise in conjunction with what our senses are telling us and what our memories recall.

Whilst understanding the significance of sensory processing is key to understanding the relationship between the mind and the design of environments, there is a risk of focusing too closely on the mechanics of sensory processing and losing sight of other factors that are at play in our mind. It is worth acknowledging, therefore, that in order to recognize and interpret what we see, hear, smell, etc., there is a degree to which our minds compare and contrast what we are sensing with what we have previously experienced in order to interpret and attribute meaning or significance to what we perceive.

Consequently, what we sense usually gives rise to metaphorical and emotional associations. So, whilst there is an objective and physical process of sensation, it is shaped by subjective interpretation. For example, many people living with dementia experience more rapid depletion of detailed memory in comparison to more visceral and emotional memories. Therefore, their interpretation of what they sense can change, such that a dark doormat on a floor may be perceived as a hole in the floor (see Figure 10.1), or shiny floors may be interpreted as being wet and slippery.

However, this 'compare and contrast' process in and of itself may not be as straightforward a process when it comes to interpreting what the senses are picking up. For example, it is thought that most people sample the emotions of others by mimicking/mirroring – much like comparing and contrasting. However, people on the autistic spectrum can find this sampling process difficult – such that they struggle to decipher the emotional and metaphorical interpretation of social signals around them.[1]

Figure 10.1 Is it a hole?

It is even thought that to some extent this mirroring process is used to apply anthropomorphic metaphors to what we perceive when inanimate objects are juxtaposed, since some juxtaposition of inanimate objects stimulates the neurological activity that is triggered by the social scenarios that these juxtapositions remind us of.[2] For example, if on inanimate object wraps around another, we may associate this with hugging.

Avoiding confusion

Since interpretation of sensory information varies and cannot always be taken as being straightforward, avoidance of confusion in environments is a key objective. For example:

- Without key locations on routes having a 'sense of place' around them, they will be harder to navigate via or to.

- Unless a doorway looks like an entrance, it will not necessarily be perceived as a 'portal' to an environment beyond.

- Some floor patterns may add further confusion by being misinterpreted as objects on the floor, as uneven or, in some cases, as steps (see Figure 10.2).

Figure 10.2 Are those steps I see?

- If a tap does not have a handle, then some people will fail to see it as a tap, especially if their longer-term visual metaphors were full of seeing taps as having cross heads.

- If a hand-wash basin is designed as a continuous trough and is too similar to a urinal, then do not be surprized if it is used by some as a urinal (in one case, signs had to be put up to say that the basin was for hand washing) (see Figure 10.3).

Figure 10.3 Wash hand basin or urinal?

Some architects and designers go out of their way to design something original but fail to recognize the significance of meaning and metaphor for those trying to understand their design. Consequently, in addition to the avoidance of stress-inducing sensory environments, avoidance of confusion is a key objective of mind-friendly and people-centric design and architecture.

Professor Joseph Giacomin[3] of the Human-Centred Design Institute at Brunel University, London, is an example of someone who takes particular interest in meaning and metaphor in his research work.

11

Reasoning, Learning and Understanding

This chapter addresses the assumption that the failure to understand an environment is down to a person rather than the environment.

Whilst people's reasoning, learning and understanding/comprehension abilities vary, it can all too often be assumed that someone's difficulty understanding an environment is because of their learning difficulty, dementia or mental illness. However, if you understand sensory triggers and the degree to which spatial configuration can confuse the most neurologically capable person, then you might start to think otherwise. This becomes particularly poignant when we understand what sensory deprivation can do to people's minds.[1]

Perception

Particularly within the realm of learning difficulties or dementia, reasoning is not always lacking if understood from a perspective and frame of reference of an individual. When you get to know individuals and have prior knowledge of a person's life, then sometimes someone's reasoning can make perfect sense. Much of this is about appreciating perception within context.

Take, for example, one of my grandmothers. Her outlook had always been one of having a cup that was half full as opposed to half empty. However, she went from being very independent to needing a lot of support from family members. This was because she suddenly lost the blood supply to her eyes and part of her brain due to a stroke, leaving her with little sight and significant short-term memory loss.

On one occasion whilst sitting in her apartment, I asked her where she thought she was at that moment in time.

She replied in her usual upbeat way, 'Oh, I'm on the train.'

To anyone who did not know her, they would have thought that she had lost her ability to reason! However, to those who knew her, it made perfect sense. Given that her memory and sight were not giving much of a clue as to where she was at that point in time and that she had worked on the railways, it made perfect sense to her and to her family. Context then becomes a matter of perspective! What clues would the design (that you are calling for, commissioning or undertaking) give as to how it is intended to be perceived or might otherwise be perceived?

Consider visual illusions and how confusing they can be. However, there are less obvious causes of confusion. Take a step back and reconsider some environments you know of from the perspective of different users. Then the lack of sensory clues, clarity and logic in a layout could be the reason for a lack of understanding for some of its users!

Language, information and communication

As has already been explained,[2] what we design gives rise to meaning and metaphor, which in turn influences reasoning and understanding. In the practice of architecture, we call this the language of architecture. For example, we can use design of doorways to evoke the sense of 'entrance' and other means to create distinctive 'places' for which we find evocative metaphors. However, single architectural 'phrases' such as these on their own only go some way in enabling the comprehension of an environment. What we should use is a string of phrases to enable wayfinding. As such, we should not just assume that comprehension of an environment happens automatically. Ironically, there are some designers who believe that their buildings 'speak for themselves'. I was once told this when visiting a building designed by an award-winning practice. Having found it difficult to navigate, I concluded that in actual fact the building failed to speak for itself and was far from self-explanatory! A designer's understanding of their own design is not always sufficiently clear to others unless they have explored and responded to how it comes across to others.

Within the separate discipline of information architecture, the user journey is really important. You could also argue that the auditory as well as the visual world should be part of this journey. How well does your environment sit within the organization's overall communication and information strategy? What pre-arrival and on-arrival information do you make available? What digital and printed information is there? How well are people being received, and how well does the overall wayfinding strategy work? What alternative communication formats are there for those with differing modes of communication or language? In other words, large and complex environments do not operate on their own. They do not function apart from the information world; if they do, then they will often fall short of their potential. After all, language, information and communication are usually at the heart of reasoning, learning and understanding.

12

Rest and Sleep

This chapter addresses how environments impact on sleep and rest.

We know from experience that our minds as well as our bodies struggle to function if we have not had opportunity to rest and to get some regular sleep.[1]

Control and choice

The usual assumption with sleep is that we need to avoid stimulation of our senses by finding somewhere warm and quiet to close our eyes and to be still. To some extent this is true, because some senses have the capability of alerting us to danger even when asleep. An appropriate environment for rest and sleep is one where we have control and in which there is no imposition of pervasive sensory stimuli. The reason for this is that we can also find rest by choosing to make elective use of our senses. People will often find listening to music,[2] exposure to the warm glow of a fire (see Figure 12.1),[3] looking at natural scenery,[4] recreational reading, smelling aromatic plants or gentle exercise/motion[5] restful. Indeed, some of us might find that such stimulation helps us get off to sleep. Design should seek to accommodate such levels of control and choice.

For example, whilst some struggle to sleep without the comfort of light, for others, avoidance of exposure to light is especially important. For some, even blackout blinds or curtains may be needed. This is because light and the relative colour of light have a time regulatory significance.[6] Moreover, furniture and bed surfaces that give us positive and yet yielding vestibular and proprioceptive support when resting or sleeping are crucial – such is the importance of furniture and bed design. We could also say that upholstery and bedding have aromatic and tactile qualities to consider. What other design choices can you think of that influence another's choices towards rest and sleep?

Figure 12.1 Warm glow of a fire

Contextual Experience

We have already established that our neurological experiences are not without context. We will now look at how different environmental factors come together to impact on our neurological processes and thus our experience.

Because context is not a wholly linear subject but a spatial one, some lateral thinking about this subject is needed. Therefore, only the first few chapters of this section have any particular sequence. The remaining chapters then seek to capture a series of environmental factors under the theme of context. Since there is an interplay between the human experience and context, and because some aspects of the human experience are more easily explained under a section heading of Contextual Experience rather the preceding section heading of The Human Experience, we will inevitably cover additional aspects of the human experience within this section (either as a prelude to explain contextual topics or as examples of how context influences the human experience).

13

Mind and Body in Context

There is much to be gained by exploring how our mind works with our body in context.

It is not uncommon for people to think of something as either being to do with our minds or with our bodies rather than seeing that mind and body are inseparable from one another. For example, from my own experience when I was a child,[1] an infant schoolteacher suggested that I might have a hearing impairment. This was then initially discounted by those undertaking hearing tests, even though it was later identified by an educational psychologist that I did indeed have a hearing impairment (yet not at the peripheral level originally tested for, but at a central level in that I had difficulties deciphering what I heard). When it came to speech therapy, because they perceived that my difficulties were not to do with the physical mechanics of speech, the speech therapists at the time decided that they could not do anything. Thankfully, we now have speech, language and communication therapy, which has a much better grasp of the neurophysiology of hearing and speaking. Would not it be great if design disciplines underwent a similar transformation in understanding how environments impact us in terms of mind and body?

Sensory deprivation

Perhaps what most powerfully demonstrates the significance of context to our mind–body make-up is what happens when we are subjected to extreme sensory deprivation. An abstract and a review of this extensively researched subject can be found in the *American Journal of Psychiatry*.[2]

On an anecdotal level, Steven Orfield,[3] who works in the realm of the senses, has an anechoic chamber at his Orfield Laboratories in Minnesota in the US (see Figure 13.1), which can be found described in the book of *Guinness World Records* as the world's quietest place, since sound insulation and sound absorbance render it an extremely 'dead' space acoustically. In a conversation between me and Stephen Orfield, Orfield mentioned that the longest amount of time people can last in the room with the lights out is not much more than 30 minutes before starting to hallucinate. This is because minds (that which we associate with thought and other attributes of personhood, which are processed via brains and the nervous system), cannot cope without the sensory input by which we reference ourselves and establish what is real and interact with that which we have established, via our senses, as being real. What is more, after a while people will have to sit down because they cannot stand up straight anymore. Similarly, according to Steven Orfield, one of the challenges for astronauts in space is the lack of external auditory input when in spacesuits. Consequentially, astronauts are exposed to being detrimentally stimulated by the sound of their own breathing and heartbeat. This is because such essential bodily processes should remain subconscious if our mind and body are to function properly. If we are too aware of such processes, then our conscious mind struggles to cope. If, as an astronaut, you are weightless in space, aspects of your tactile (touch), vestibular (balance) and proprioception (positioning) functioning will be further deprived of sensory input due to weightlessness.

Figure 13.1 Anechoic chamber at Orfield Labs
Image provided by Steven Orfield

Sensory overload

The subject of sensory overload has also been researched extensively. For example, Sensory Integration Education has collated the evidence pertaining to this and other aspects of sensory processing on their website.[4]

According to conversations with Steven Orfield, whilst sensory deprivation occurs in extreme environments, other usually unnoticed sources of stimulus become amplified, and people subjected to sensory deprivation start hearing things like their own repetitive heartbeat or breathing. Ironically, this then leads to sensory overload – especially as repetitive sounds are harder to block out. It stands to reason, then, that when it comes to external sources of sensory noise that we are involuntarily subjected to (usually auditory, visual and sometimes olfactory), our minds may struggle to function through stress, confusion and anxiety. This has been identified by those undertaking research in sensory integration (and other related fields).[5]

The bandwidth for digital data on our broadband service is a useful analogy to sensory overload. Some of what we experience with sensory overload is like when we are trying to stream lots of data down a narrow bandwidth, and everything then slows down. So, for some of us, it is as though we either have too narrow a bandwidth for certain forms of sensory processing or that our sensory processing gives rise to so much data that we cannot quite cope with what bandwidth we have left. From brain imaging studies that have been undertaken on some people on the autistic spectrum (such as Temple Grandin)[6] we might conclude that this issue for some of us is the latter – with too much 'data' firing at once through our brains to cope with – unless we develop our own personal strategies for managing this sensory information.

When you reflect on the challenges posed by sensory overload or sensory deprivation, you soon realize how crucial our sensory environments are to our neurological wellbeing and you will begin to perceive how interconnected we are with our environments.

Other dimensions

There are other dimensions to what we experience.

- One dimension is time. We will later take a look at how context has a significant relationship to how our memories function.[7] This relates to how our senses are working in time and context.

- Another is a social dimension. Whilst our physical environment is the primary source of sensory input, it is also the context for our social environment, which comes with complex and dynamic sensory inputs and outputs. Our social environment is framed by how our physical environment is designed and configured. For example, we often use socially significant words such as private, intimate, secluded, secure, open, exposed and crowded to describe how spaces impact on our social interactions. Where there is a lack of choice in space, we can reasonably expect stress to occur in order to make an adjustment according to our social need.

- Yet another dimension is human diversity. We do not all process our senses in the same way. It is now recognized by most educationalists that people will differ in their learning styles – which are in effect their thinking and sensory profiles.

This is where our thoughts are stimulated and motivated differently and to varying degrees by visual, auditory, kinaesthetic, group and individual learning styles. One can also surmise that taste and smell have an influence on our thought processes and therefore our learning processes too, although perhaps more subconsciously.[8]

Context phobias and phenomena

Some context-based phobias[9] and phenomena, such as agoraphobia (the fear of open spaces), claustrophobia (the fear of confined spaces), acrophobia (the fear of heights), monophobia (the fear of being alone), cabin fever and a plethora of other contextual phenomena can perhaps begin to be understood in terms of the social, spatial and physical context of different environmental scenarios and the challenges posed by the sensory environment. Human-centric design becomes a consideration of choice of environments and opportunities in which people might find space in which they might function best at any given time.

14

Spatial Context

The spatial environment around us provides our minds with both context and the source of stimuli.

Where environments are subject to human intervention and design, these environments will present particular implications for our minds, over and above those of the natural environment. Most of these implications arise from what has been provided in the way of sensory ingredients, which we will summarize here and go into in more detail about in later chapters.

Auditory ingredients[1]

Auditory stimulus from the environment about us comes as a result of sound. Sound is usually a significant ingredient of communication but can have a significant effect on our neurological processes and emotions too. The acoustics of an environment play an important role in how we function – in terms of not only thinking and communicating but also enjoyment.

Sound can be decipherable and it can be wanted or unwanted, whether decipherable or not. What turns into distracting noise depends as much on the tasks/goals one has in a given moment as on the external factors. The same holds true for any sense.

Visual ingredients[2]

Our visual sense is the principal sense by which we perceive spaces around us. As with sound, the visual realm can also give rise to decipherable and wanted stimulus or unwanted noise.

Visual stimulus from the environment around us comes from light, surfaces (visual treatment in the form of colour, patterns and illumination), the configuration of the space (whether internal or external) and what is in the space.

Since vision is one of our major senses, the visual environment will also have a significant impact on our minds – either directly through the interplay of our sensory and our neurological processes, via our emotions or indirectly through its role in communication and wayfinding.

Respiratory ingredients[3]

Air quality is an especially important ingredient; after all, our brains need oxygen to function. Not only this, but an excess of other gases, such as carbon dioxide, has an effect on blood chemistry with a consequential adverse effect on the brain. Some other pollutants in the air will also have adverse effects on the brain when inhaled. The design of building ventilation is especially important.

Aromatic ingredients[4]

Buildings, landscapes and urban environments are the sources of all sorts of aromas. Smells arise from plants, the activities that go on in and around buildings, natural and synthetic building materials and cleaning materials. Smell can be quite a powerful sense in that we can often associate smells either with pleasurable things like foods that we like or with substances (including some foods) we do not like or substances of a noxious nature. Smell has significant scope to alert us, put us at ease or impinge on our thoughts in other ways.

Gustatory ingredients[5]

Environments in which we find ourselves can be the contexts in which we find and consume food, thereby exercising our gustatory sense along with our olfactory sense, with all the positive and negative implications that this has for our sensory processing and emotional and thought processes. Consequently, the availability of food- and drink-related facilities has neurological implications, which we should be aware of when environments are designed. However, it is worth noting that some people (such as some children and adults on the autistic spectrum) have the urge to place inappropriate substances into their mouths. When it comes to designing specialist environments, it is important to design out hazards whilst considering safe and positive gustatory opportunities.

Tactile ingredients[6]

Surfaces and objects that we come into contact with are the means by which we exercise our tactile sense. We gain tactile sensations when we walk across different surfaces which in turn influence how we move. Otherwise, tactile and related sensations are, more often than not, sensations of choice rather than imposition and a means by which we investigate environments with our hands. An additional form of tactile investigation is when we place materials against our cheeks (maybe taking in the smell and surface temperature of that material at the same time). And there is yet one deeper form of interaction: when we enfold ourselves in a manner that yields the sensory reassurance of deep pressure. As with taste, some people (such as some children and adults on the autistic spectrum) can place inappropriate things in their mouths for tactile reasons too.

Proprioceptive and vestibular ingredients[7]

Much like exercising our tactile and deep pressure senses, the means to exercise our proprioception (body positioning) and our vestibular (balance) senses are usually ones of opportunity rather than direct imposition. However, when there is no choice, it will feel like imposition or deprivation. Hence, the choice of furniture is important in terms of how it provides for different proprioception and vestibular needs at any given point in time. The availability or otherwise of recreational facilities is also important in this regard.

Whilst these two senses are amongst the least well known within the wider population, it is important to recognize the significance that sensory integration specialists place on them when it comes to regulating neurological processes and enabling minds to function. What to some may seem inconsequential in design terms could have significant design implications.

Indeed, we know from experience that in addition to the role the inner ear plays, balance is affected by what we see. But do we appreciate how much some people's balance can be affected? I have received reports of people's balance being affected by an askew bridge enclosure in Bristol, including a report from a member of my own family (see Figure 14.1).

In one school of architecture, several students reported to me that the vertical wooden battens on a black background within their university studio were enough to make them feel dizzy (see Figure 14.2). One person even described to me how they could not talk whilst walking down stairs in which there were similar and even more vertical lines occurring. One could surmise that their mind was so taken up by the visual noise, there was only sufficient brain capacity left to walk rather than talk as well.

Figure 14.1 This bridge in Bristol is known to affect people's balance

Figure 14.2 People feel dizzy with this pattern

The disturbing thing here is the potential implication for safety. Take, for example, another flight of stairs known to me, where in addition to there being lots of repetitive vertical balustrade rails, treads are not in a straight line, they consist of a busy pattern and alcohol is frequently consumed in the building.

At another university, one student described to me how highly-contrasting paving pattern on the campus, induced a sense of vertigo. Again, this was corroborated by one of my own family reporting a similar experience. It was also easy to see how the pattern could be perceived as steps, especially by partially sighted people. The pattern, when viewed on approach, could be considered visually noisy (see Figure 14.3). These two additional factors could also have implications for maintaining balance, too.

Figure 14.3 Problematic paving pattern: perception of steps, vertigo and visual noise

Thermal ingredients[8]

Whilst we can usually make personal adjustments for thermal comfort, the environments that we design have a significant effect on how comfortable we feel and consequentially how our minds work. We know that extreme temperature conditions such as hypothermia and heat stroke can have very adverse effects on our brain's ability to function, let alone on the usual sensory processing and integration aspects of temperature. Temperature regulation is not always that easy, and some people find it difficult to know what the temperature is and become susceptible to overheating or becoming too cold and not quite finding the point at which they feel 'just right'.

The chronometric ingredient[9]

How we place ourselves in time is significantly affected by our ability to track changes in our environment on a daily basis. Whilst seasonal changes will help augment our ability to track to progress of time, it is the effect that light has on our daily circadian rhythm that helps our brains regulate our activities. Our ability to function effectively will relate not only to the opportunity that our environment provides us in terms of keeping track of the progression of daylight, but also to how artificial light works with or against our circadian rhythm.

The natural world[10]

Whilst the environment around us gives rise to a whole range of sensory stimulus, it is perhaps worth identifying a crucial distinction between the characteristics of different sensory signals. Indeed, it seems that for many of us, our minds are better attuned to natural rather than built environments; therefore, artificial environments when it comes to visual stimulus. Consequently, commissioning and designing environments where nature is either predominant or encouraged can have a notable impact on people's wellbeing.

Choice

Whilst not every environment suits everyone, from a neurological needs perspective, the aim should be to commission and design environments that are not bland, enable people to use them for their intended purpose, are as stress free as possible and provide different sensory opportunities within different spaces.

15

Social Context

In this chapter we connect the sensory world with social context and the added challenges and opportunities this presents.

The social world

In addition to spatial environments providing context for our minds, the social environment provides added context in which our minds operate. Usually, the social environment occurs within a specific spatial context; however, as information and communication technology have developed, the relationship between spatial and social context has become more fragmented, especially as people have taken to telecommunications, digital communication and social media. Nevertheless, spatial context remains a factor, even if we are using digital devices to communicate, as we always use such devices within a context.

What is important to note is that in sensory processing and integration terms, social sources of sensory stimulus can be especially complicated. That stimulus is likely to be impacted by the physical or information environment we find ourselves in. Within the social context, not only are we having to process sensory signals from the environment around us when we meet people, but we are also having to detect subtle differences in people's facial expressions, body language and tone of voice. This is assuming that we are not using telecommunications or digital communication, where the task of interpretation can be made harder by the removal of one or more of the sensory signals that we use in communication. For some, reducing sensory input helps but comes at the risk of users experiencing 'virtual autism' (whether they are on the autistic spectrum or not) when tone of voice and facial expressions are removed and only text is used. For me, however, digital devices enable me to spell check and order my thoughts, becoming for me the dyslexic's equivalence of wearing a pair of spectacles.

Mirroring and communication

In order to interact with one another, we usually need to be able to mirror the expressions of others so that we not only decipher what they are saying on an informational level but also detect what they are saying on an emotional level. We tend to micro-mimic others in order to sample their emotion as we interact (see Figure 15.1).[1] Communication is such a source of stimulus; it is so complex, that we can either find ourselves seeking out stimuli that we get from social interaction with others or needing 'time out' because of the sheer sensory overload that we can experience. However, some people find expressing emotions and mirroring difficult to do, to the extent that some people on the autistic spectrum will present few facial clues to enable a person to detect their emotions. Interestingly enough, it is thought that Botox treatment, which paralyzes facial muscles, may make it harder for people to empathize with others.[2]

Figure 15.1 Mirroring reflects expression

It also seems that the neurological mirroring processes involve interpreting that which we see around us anthropomorphically.[3] This way of thinking will also influence the adjectives that we use to describe an environment (see Figure 15.2).[4] For example, we tend to see windows as a building's eyes and see windowless walls as unseeing. Such anthropomorphic adjectives also help us to gain further insight about how our embodied minds relate to the environment about us. I recall a structures lecturer who encouraged his students get a sense of how forces in a structure worked by imagining themselves as an element of that structure.

Figure 15.2 The greyed-out windows at Bristol's Royal Infirmary are unfriendly, in addition to the visually noisy patterning of the fenestration

Choice of space

Because we all differ and our need for social stimulus varies from one person to another, environments need to be designed in order to facilitate choice and accommodate different forms of social interaction. Some spaces need to facilitate being alone. Others need to facilitate one-to-one or small group interactions, whilst others need to facilitate larger groups. On one hand, the lack of opportunity to socialize will hinder our wellbeing, whilst not being able to 'find our own space' will hinder us too.

Space bubbles and proxemics

Many of us can identify with the sensation we feel when someone is 'in our space' or even 'in our face'. This sensation occurs when someone has crossed 'that invisible line' between what is an acceptable distance and what is not acceptable. However, this distance varies according to personalities, the relationship and the situation. In other words, there is no set distance of 'too close' because that distance is determined by the mind of the individual. The distance will tend to relate to our level of familiarity with the other person. It will also relate to a perceived level of threat and the available space that there is in a given environment. For example, when there are not many people around in an urban area or parkland after dark, we may wish to give strangers a wide berth or avoid the area all together. On the other hand, in an environment like a crowded pub, we might find that we can tolerate others being in what would otherwise be 'our' space, because we are prepared to make that adjustment in exchange for the social opportunity.

In architecture we refer to this phenomenon as proxemics or people's 'space bubbles' (see Figure 15.3) – bubbles that change in size – a theory developed by Edward T. Hall in the '60s.[5] We can usually see proxemics at work in restaurants and meeting places, where the distribution of people tends to be fairly even when people start to arrive and choose their preferred seating. As more people arrive, they have little alternative other than filling the gaps.

Figure 15.3 Space bubbles tell us when others are too close

What is worth noting, therefore, is that the practice of architecture and related design disciplines involves setting boundaries, containment of activities and 'framing' the lives we live out.[6] One way we can help people to relax and avoid the threat of people invading their space bubbles is by paying attention to what makes people feel secure and/or relaxed.[7] For some individuals, their space bubbles might be larger than average. As such, if we are to cater for different scenarios and people's diverse needs, then it is always worth considering a range of spatial opportunities for different social or even individual opportunities.

16

Comfort and Activity

This chapter identifies the relationship between our minds and our tactile, proprioception and vestibular and senses in the context of physical activity and comfort.

Movement

There is usually nothing quite like walking/moving from one place to another to help refresh our minds, especially if we need to think something through or to step away from a task in order to get some 'headspace'. This, in part, is because walking provides us with an opportunity to exercise and integrate sensory processes. Whilst efficient and physically accessible circulation routes through and within environments are important, the opportunity for simple exercise through walking, cycling or using a wheelchair is also important for our minds. For example, there is a growing awareness of the beneficial effects of walking and other physical activities for individuals living with dementia.[1] Means by which we move around environments, such as open space, paths, gradients, ramps, steps, stairs and corridors, provide us with valuable opportunities to exercise our proprioceptive and vestibular senses. But it is not just our proprioceptive and vestibular senses that enable us to benefit from movement. Other senses are also stimulated.

- As we walk, our tactile sense is stimulated via our feet.

- Vision is also stimulated as we move around and when what we see then changes. So important is movement to vision and the brain that if something were to prevent the natural oscillating movement of the eyeball, the brain switches our vision off![2] If stationary, we also tend to move our heads from side to side to further stimulate the sense of depth in our field of vision. By deduction it is possible to understand how walking, cycling and using a wheelchair adds further beneficial visual stimulation to our minds.

- We also have the opportunity to detect changes in sound and smell. Not only this, but we may also have the opportunity to exercise our gustatory and tactile senses if we choose to forage!

As such, the activity of walking/movement can become a refreshing multisensory activity, provided that the environment itself does not present too much in the way of sensory overload. The right kind of multisensory stimulation has the potential to offer minds a thorough refresh.

Furniture

We do not have occasion to be on the move all the time, and therefore when we are stationary we are usually reliant on the furniture to not only provide us with tactile comfort and deep-pressure comfort but also enable us to exercise our proprioceptive and vestibular senses.

If you have ever wondered why some people like to rock and balance on the back of four-legged chairs, it is usually because their minds are looking for the sensory stimulation that this provides. Rocking chairs and ergonomically designed office chairs (that allow us to move around and lean backwards) can yield significant benefits through sensory stimulus.[3]

The opportunity to use standing desks for part of the time whilst working in offices is usually seen as beneficial to our circulation and muscular/skeletal frame. Standing desks could also yield proprioceptive and vestibular sensory processing benefits as well. Sometimes, however, we may just want the opportunity to sit back in a cosy sofa or armchair surrounded by pillows. The key is not necessarily one thing or another but, instead, offering choice.

It is also worth mentioning that it is all too easy for there to be limited choice with regard to the height of chairs and whether the chairs have arm rests or not. There are significant benefits to be had by being able to adjust desk heights as well. In other words, if there is a lack of attention to people's muscular/skeletal comfort, one can hardly expect their minds to be working well too.

Facilities

Given the importance of getting exercise for both our physical and mental health, you might consider purposeful inclusion of both internal and external and exercise facilities that can be accessed by people with diverse physical and neurological needs. Could workplaces yield productivity benefits for staff engaged in regular exercise?

Choice of opportunity

Because sensory vestibular and proprioceptive processing needs vary from one person to another, the way in which environments are designed needs to accommodate different forms of activity, furniture and facilities. In other words, we need a variety of opportunities.

17

Acoustics

This chapter examines the relationship between our minds and our auditory senses.

Pervasive sound

Whilst some people have minds that can filter out background sounds, this is not always a straightforward task for everyone. Whilst with sight we can usually close our eyes or avert our gaze, when it comes to our auditory sense we do not usually have an immediate physiological means of avoiding auditory stimuli other than placing objects or our hands over our ears. This is very possibly because hearing is a residual sense when it comes to detecting danger, such as when we are asleep or when we cannot see danger. It is perhaps significant that the medical profession considers the auditory sense as important when people seem otherwise disconnected from the world around them when in a coma. Consequently, soundscape is crucial for our minds to function either in terms of thinking or actually communicating. Hearing therefore not only involves the physiological processes of the ears but also involves sensory processing and integration. The emergent discipline of psychoacoustics involves the study of psychological implications of sound. For example, Dr Nigel Oseland is a psychologist who takes particular interest in this field and its application to workplaces.[1]

There are several things to take account of when thinking about an environment's acoustics. First, there is the sound at source and what the volume, pitch, direction and pattern are. Second, is it decipherable sound that can be interpreted as music, speech or some other code? Does it constitute noise to the hearer (in that it is distracting, annoying or unpleasant) whether it is decipherable or indecipherable?

Whilst sound is important for communication and enjoyment of music, volume, pitch and pattern of sound can engender different reactions. Take alarms for example – we quite definitely have a neurological response to these sounds. However, there are some sounds, especially repetitive sounds such as dripping taps, that can easily become unbearable for some (despite other people remaining unaware), especially when they want to concentrate, work out what others are saying or just 'switch off' and rest or sleep.

Communication

Moreover, when it comes to communicating, deciphering speech is an extraordinarily complex process, requiring our brains to make sense of what we hear. As speech uses vowel and consonant sounds, some sounds are easier to hear then others. As we get older, we learn to fill in the gaps in speech when acoustics prevent us from hearing vowel sounds. However, children and some adults will lack the experience and or ability to fill in the gaps. Sound therefore has an important function and can be a means of enjoyment, distraction or discomfort, but it can also be a means of deciphering meaning from the soundscape around us.

Singing and music

It is worth noting that acoustics form the backdrop to another noteworthy vocal activity: singing and music. Whilst communication in itself is functionally important to human activity, singing and music have additional significant neurological benefits.

Studies have indicated that when people sing, they show signs of an increased sense of wellbeing, bonding and trust, combined with a reduction in stress, which is indicated on a hormonal level by increased levels of endorphins, increased levels of oxytocin and reduced levels of cortisol.[2] It also seems that singing may help regulate heart rates and that musical memory lasts longer than other memories. People living with dementia have been observed remembering songs when they have lost the ability to remember other things. Dr A. D. Patel says, 'Music provides a way to access regions of the brain and reawaken memory when language simply won't.'[3] Not only this, but some people also who have difficulty speaking, who have had a stroke,[4] who are living with dementia[5] or who are on the autistic spectrum[6] seem to be able to vocalize with greater ease when singing.

It stands for reason, therefore, that making environments available that foster and encourage song and music will be beneficial. These spaces are not necessarily those that are conducive to spoken communication, as spaces with longer reverberation times are often better for singing or playing music. For example, I once played hymns, choruses and Hebraic tunes on my Eb Tenor Horn in a tunnel beneath a local railway, where the acoustics were conducive and where passers-by regularly smiled and expressed their enjoyment, not infrequently recognizing the tunes. This is not surprising, since Isaiah 61:3 (NKJV) says, 'The oil of joy for mourning. The garment or praise for the spirit of heaviness.'

Choice of acoustics: calm and stimulating

Calm environments with the choice of obtaining auditory stimuli are a good place to start when thinking about acoustics from a neurological perspective. Creating calm environments includes:

- removing sources of noise or providing separation from sources of noise (often one of the most desirable considerations, especially for internal environments)

- achieving the right balance between sound attenuation and reflection.

This is because there are critical situations where background sound and very reverberant spaces can cause problems for the activities within. Essentially this is when we are either endeavouring to communicate, such as at receptions points, in classrooms or other locations where there is a transfer of auditory information. The other scenario is when we are trying to concentrate or rest. A valuable source of information on the subject of acoustics is a document called BB93: Acoustic Design of Schools – Performance Standards.[7] When we are navigating, especially if we have a visual impairment, we also use acoustic information to 'perceive' the world around us and to identify where we are. However, it is important to remember the importance of calm environments and wherever possible to avoid imposing auditory stimulus that is pervasive (and difficult to filter out) in areas that are intended for communication, work or rest.

Calm environments should therefore be designed in a manner that leads to reduction of noise and clear interpretation of sound and speech and should enable people with hearing impairments and neurological needs (such as dyslexia and other learning or language difficulties) to have a reasonable likelihood of making optimum use of the speech that they are endeavouring to hear, decipher or 'decode'.

We also need stimulating environments, since at the most basic level we struggle to function if there is virtually no sound at all such as in an anechoic chamber.[8] It is therefore worth making spaces available where clear communication is not required and where reverberation times are either just stimulating or necessary to enjoy music and singing.

Achieving stimulating acoustics can also be an aim in landscape design, such as making use of water features, rustling leaves, human activity or bird sounds. There are also occasions where indoor sound is sought, since some of us might like to 'bathe' in the soundscapes of places like cafés or put some music on in spaces we inhabit.

Components of acoustics

Some design considerations may require the assistance of an acoustic consultant, whilst some can be readily understood with less acoustic knowledge and early thought about how environments are set out. In order to achieve choice for people with different auditory needs, designers will need to consider basic acoustic principles, such as:

- purpose and function of alternative spaces being designed

- sound projection and sound containment according to whether sound is wanted or not

- identification and location of unwanted noise sources – both internally and externally to a building and according to layout of spaces within (proximity to sound sources)

- separation of spaces that generate noise from sound-sensitive spaces (see Figure 17.1)

Figure 17.1 Sound separation – removing source of noise by distance

- sound paths such as through construction, service ducts and circulation routes

- sound insulation (resistance to sound through construction) through wall, partition, door and glazing specifications (see Figure 17.2)

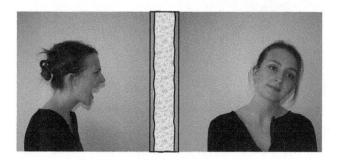

Figure 17.2 Sound insulation – reducing sound transmission between adjacent spaces

- flanking details (locations where sound might go around an element of insulation) (see Figure 17.3)

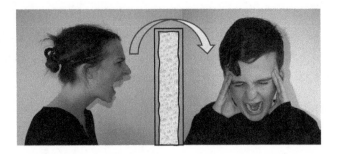

Figure 17.3 Flanking sound – when sound finds a path

- sound attenuation (absorption of sound through surfaces) on potential sound paths and reducing reverberation in spaces through the choice of building elements, fixtures, finishes and furniture (too much attenuation is uncomfortable to our ears and too little causes too much reverberation and consequential accumulative noise) (see Figure 17.4)

Figure 17.4 Sound attenuation – absorbing sound within a space
Background image provided by Stephen Orfield

- sound reflection (bouncing of sound off hard surfaces)

- reverberation (the degree to which resonance is maintained in a space) (see Figure 17.5)

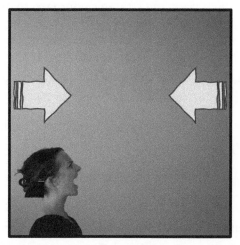

Figure 17.5 Sound reflection and reverberation
– sustaining sound within a space

- sound enhancement through sound field systems, induction loops, infrared and radio systems.

Assistive technology

You should also seriously consider a sound field amplification system within classrooms, large meeting rooms and auditoria because:

- It enables children and young people to pick up more of the component parts of speech and therefore comprehend better what is being said and better pay attention.

- It greatly benefits people with hearing difficulties, learning difficulties, language difficulties and behavioural difficulties.

- It reduces the risk of speakers straining their voices.

- It reduces the sense of isolation that people with hearing impairments can experience and the emotional and other potential psychological effects of such isolation.

For similar reasons, a clear and strategic approach to other hearing assistance should be employed where:

- Induction loops are provided at counters and in receptions, meeting rooms, event spaces and adjacent to communication devices (such as call points and intercoms).

- Portable infrared should also be provided elsewhere, especially where privacy is needed.

- Radio-based equipment should be used if neither of the above are suitable.

- Captioning and audio description can also help with regard to people's hearing, sight and communication difficulties.

18

Lighting

This chapter addresses the relationship between our minds and our visual and time senses within the context of lighting.

Beyond illumination

Light is what enables us to see the world around us when we have use of our eyes. Light also helps us keep track of time and therefore has an important neurological function. On one hand it illuminates what we see and on the other hand it helps regulate our circadian rhythm and enables us to know what time it is and whether rest or activity is what we ought to be doing.[1]

It is thought that light plays a contributory part in time regulation by data being processed through more than one part of the brain. For example, people with dementia can find it difficult to sleep when exposed to light during the night and they benefit from blackout curtains and no lighting at all when trying to sleep. Moreover, people with Parkinson's disease, attention difficulties or hyperactivity issues are thought have difficulties with how parts of their brain function in relation to time.[2] It is known that some people on the autistic spectrum, or who experience migraines or epilepsy, find it easier to function where lighting is constant and not subject to an alternating pulse.[3] There is also thought to be a relationship between seasonal changes in light and depression experienced by people with seasonal affective disorder.[4]

Choice of lighting: calm and stimulus

As with acoustics, visually calm environments with a choice and variety of visual stimuli are a good place to start when thinking about lighting from a neurological perspective, provided that intense visual stimulus is a choice and is not imposed in areas that are intended for everyone.

Natural light

Other than a few exceptions (such as moonlight, starlight and biochemical light), natural light in the main comes in two forms. Daylight is the background light of the day, which originates from the sun but is the indirect and diffused or reflected component of natural light. Sunlight is direct light from the sun and is very intense and directional. During the day, light changes in different colours according to what angle it passes through the atmosphere. It is this change in colour during the day that is thought to help regulate our circadian rhythm, with the warmer light of the mornings and evenings being more conducive to a restful state of mind and the colder and bluer light being more conducive to stimulating activity. Consequently, bluer light during the evening is likely to make us feel tired.[5]

Making good use of daylight and sunlight are important factors in designing environments, whether they are landscapes, urban realms or buildings. The ability to not only harnesses daylight and sunlight but to control and manage how they enter the building is a critical design consideration.

Of the two, sunlight is usually welcome if one enables it to enter a design at higher elevations but becomes more problematic if it enters at lower elevations, where our eyes have difficulty adjusting to its intensity. For some individuals, adjusting to intense daylight can be problematic. I have witnessed someone I know having a sudden seizure when they were caught unawares by sunlight.

Good, natural daylight, because it is dispersed indirect light and changes colour during the day, and with a means of adjusting light levels, provides a calm backdrop to many an environment. Providing shading from sunlight and canopies from intense daylight with things like awnings and roller blinds are positive design features to include wherever possible. However, alternating shadow patterns can have an impact in terms of inducing greater cognitive load.[6] Daylight can be a beneficial ingredient in the design of a building.

Artificial light

Whilst natural light is usually preferable, artificial light usually cannot be avoided in the design of buildings. However, there are things that you can do to enhance people's experiences and reduce problems caused by some artificial lighting. The considerations of human-centric lighting[7] are an indication of the importance of lighting design beyond illumination calculations alone.

Artificial lighting has a bearing on everyone's ability to navigate and use an environment, but has particular implications for people with visual impairments, people with hearing impairments who lip read and people with neurological needs. Some people with particular neurological needs also have intolerances to light of certain frequencies, colours and intensity.

Good lighting that avoids excessive reflection, glare and shadowing and provides good quality illumination should therefore contribute to:

- visual and architectural clarity

- identification of routes, entrances and elements

- clear colour and contrast rendering of built elements

- the clarity of signage and information.

Inclusive design decisions should inform the choice of:

- background lighting design

- task lighting design

- lighting output levels of lamps

- illumination levels

- colour temperatures.

Light where one needs it

Natural and artificial lighting design should avoid casting shadows onto work surfaces and causing glare. What might not cause significant glare to some people could cause real problems for people with visual and neurological difficulties.

Lighting also needs to be conducive to those who rely on lip reading and signing and needs to be such that awkward shadows are not cast across faces. Remember that even if a person does not have a hearing impairment, most find it easier to understand others at a neurological level when we integrate body language, facial expressions and lip movements and thereby visually reinforce what we hear.

Lighting schemes that combine more than one form of lighting to provide good background lighting combined with lighting for specific tasks work best. Light fittings and light sources should address the ergonomic relationship between the lighting source and task position whilst taking care of glare reduction, colour rendering and facial modelling.

Good practice for background lighting would be to use up-lighting, combined with a well-defused down-lighting element and specific task lighting; Wall-mounted bulkhead light fittings can give rise to glare problems, since they can be in the line of sight. Spotlights can also be problematic, unless targeted at a wall or object in such a way that they are unlikely to shine into someone's eyes. Up-lighters on stairs can also give rise to problems since it is possible to see into the luminaire from above.

Ambient, general or background lighting needs to be good, but will not always be suitable for given tasks and particular individuals, such that there should be scope to locally control light through blinds and task lighting. Scope for making adjustments, so that lighting can be set at the optimum, helps individuals with particular lighting needs. This might include adjustment to colour output either during the day or for some individuals or groups.

Transition and external lighting

Natural and artificial lighting intensities could also be stepped up or down for areas where people are transferring to and from outdoor and indoor environments. In practice this means that artificial lighting needs to be capable of switching between downward steps in intensity during the daytime and an upward step in intensity during night times.

In external environments bulkhead lights or path-side bollard lights can cause problems, as the light source is seen as a brilliant point source in the context of a dark, night-time ambient environment. It is therefore important that lights in external environments are down-lighters and are concentrated on surfaces, without causing glare or excessive pooling. Good, inclusive external lighting should also be beneficial for security purposes and for the reduction of light pollution.

Light and navigation

Lighting could also contribute to wayfinding and provide clues that assist people whilst navigating environments by:

- taking into account the needs of people with neurological needs as well as people with visual, hearing and mobility/stamina/dexterity needs

- highlighting information and routes

- warning of – or steering people from – hazards

- leading people to places of safety in an emergency

- facilitating lip reading and the deciphering of signing (including BSL and Makaton)

- being available to and from a point of arrival, via an accessible route to a place of reception and key facilities, with particular attention to parking areas, toilets, stairs and lifts

- avoiding visually bland environments that lack distinction between elements, zones or departments.

Lighting problems

Lighting should be designed so as to avoid excessive visually 'busy' illumination, reflections, glare, pooling, silhouettes and shadowing, all of which can cause particular problems for people with dementia, or those on the autistic spectrum, with brain injury and with migraine in addition to people with visual impairments (see Figure 18.1). This means avoiding:

- small light sources that can be looked into, i.e., the top of up-lighters when descending stairs, spotlights that are not targeted at walls and bollard-type lighting, which places small light sources within the visual field and inhibits vision

- recessed reflective lighting fittings and grids that do not illuminate ceilings directly, thereby creating oppressive and dark ceilings and upper walls, either requiring alternative light fittings or additional light sources

- casting shadows across steps and inadvertently leading people into danger or preventing them seeing or perceiving danger

- intense lighting and lighting that runs the risk of strobing within a frequency band that is likely to cause problems for people with epilepsy and those on the autistic spectrum

- light fittings with poor colour output

- fluorescent light wherever possible, using high-frequency fittings if there is no alternative

- some LED lights unless they are well controlled centrally on a direct current circuit and where their intense point source light is diffused

- visual alarms, unless there is no safe alternative and only then if they pulsate simultaneously on the same circuit and at a combined frequency that is least problematic.

Figure 18.1 Glare- and visual noise-inducing lighting

Some of the bigger lighting problems are likely to be the greatest outdoors. For example, glare-related problems are much greater outdoors during the night, since skies and backgrounds are dark, resulting in light sources appearing much more intense.

19

Surfaces

This chapter addresses the relationship between our minds and senses within the context of surfaces, patterns, colours and textures.

Form and space perception

Apart from my conviction that architecture should be practiced as a form of service design, architecture is essentially the art of manipulating form and space. However, the interfaces between form and space are surfaces – perceived by our visual, tactile and auditory senses. These surfaces define the envelope of both the forms and spaces with which we co-exist in order that we may perceive the three-dimensional context of our existence.

Auditory surface perception

Although our visual and tactile senses are our primary senses in detecting surface, form and space, our auditory sense can also assist us in understanding characteristics about the spaces we are in. Our auditory sense also enables us to perceive something about the surfaces within these spaces. If we are enclosed by hard surfaces, we can sometimes perceive the nature of both the surfaces in these spaces and how large these spaces are through the time it takes for sound to either bounce back as an echo or remain present in a space through reverberation.

Some individuals who have lost their sight have, in exceedingly rare circumstances, even developed sonar-like abilities through how their minds have processed and integrated sensory information – even being able to perceive the position of objects in a space.[1] Sound absorption, however, diminishes the scope for our auditory senses to perceive the surfaces, spaces and forms around us. Nevertheless, if we are endeavouring to decipher speech, some such sound absorption helps us to separate speech from background noise. This is especially important for people with hearing impairments, but it also helps people with auditory processing difficulties (such as those experienced by me).

Sound absorption is a characteristic of soft and textured surfaces, whereas reverberation is a characteristic of hard and smoother surfaces. It is our tactile and visual senses that help confirm what our ears are hearing and provide our minds with the means by which this auditory information is integrated to the point that we can make sense of what the sound is telling us about the environment around us.

Tactile surface perception

Touch is often a choice, except when we are walking or have to reach out for something. The tactile nature of surfaces can tell us quite a lot about a space and can even be used underfoot to alert people with visual impairments as to what to expect in urban environments. When it comes to buildings, the most prominent tactile experiences are usually whilst interacting with door handles, taps, furniture and floor surfaces. The nature and design of door handles can also tell us quite a bit about what we might expect of the space that lies beyond. Ironically, the less ergonomic a door handle is, the more pretentious and exclusive the space beyond seems to be!

The degree to which we seek or avoid tactile sensations will vary from person to person. Some individuals on the autistic spectrum will either have a particular aversion to, or particular affinity with, certain tactile sensations. Indeed, deep-pressure, tactile, proprioceptive and vestibular sensations feature in sensory integration therapy. Nevertheless, it is worth understanding how furniture design might also be used to help support people at a sensory and neurological processing level too.

Our tactile senses are not able to tell us anything about colour other than perhaps as a clue to what we already know. We might associate something that is very cold and hard with translucent ice and something that is very cold and soft with white snow. If we touch something that is hot, we might associate it with the colour red. Likewise, if we touch something that has the shape and texture of a leaf, we might reasonably assume that it is green (even though it is not uncommon for leaves to occur in other colours). In each case, it is not the tactile sense itself that is telling us what colour something is but our mind drawing on experiences that our other senses have taught us. Moreover, these experiences will come with early emotions and varying abilities to cope with different tactile senses.

Visual surface perception

Of all our senses it is perhaps the visual sense for which the surfaces around us have the most significance. After all, without surfaces to illuminate, not even light has much benefit for our visual sense. However, surfaces, whether flat, rough, defining a single object or comprising multiple objects (like leaves on a tree), provide our visual sensation with both colour and patterns. We could call these colours and patterns 'signals', which have own frequency and a need for us to interpret them.

Surface patterns

We know, even from observing optical illusions, that patterns can play tricks on our minds. There is also evidence that some regular patterns can cause our minds to have problems (see Figures 19.1–19.5).

Figure 19.1 High-frequency carpet pattern giving rise to visual noise

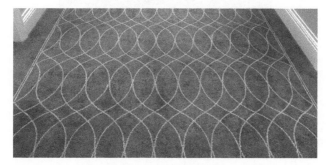

Figure 19.2 Carpet pattern with optical illusion of undulations

Figure 19.3 Visually confusing floor – reflections,
optical illusion and visually noisy pattern

Figure 19.4 Visually busy paving pattern giving rise to visual noise

Figure 19.5 Visually busy mesh curtain casting visually busy shadow on floor

According to the work of Professor Arnold Wilkins[2] and others, it seems that highly repetitive patterns that appear at a certain frequency in our visual field have the tendency to grab the attention of our minds and take up significant cognitive capacity. A pattern that repeats itself three times within a single degree of our visual field has the greatest potential to grab our mind's attention as unwanted noise. Distance from the pattern will determine the frequency. Since a degree equates roughly to one thumb width when a hand is stretched at arm's length, there is a simple means of determining whether a pattern could be problematic. Additionally, the greater the contrast of colour or tone in a pattern, the greater the effect.

Although further research is needed, it is thought that some patterns may lead to people falling. However, it appears that our minds are usually positively affected by natural patterns where the multiple frequencies have the tendency to cancel one another out. We are also better able to filter, passively engage with and even find positive stimulus from natural patterns.

The consequence of getting patterns wrong is that some minds will be negatively affected.[3] We also know that people living with dementia can find that patterns they see can act as such a strong metaphor that they derive meaning and interpretation that is not necessarily there. For example, a contrast between floor colours or tones can be perceived as a step. Sometimes patterns on floors can be perceived as objects or dark mats on light floors can be perceived as holes. Moreover, reflective, shiny surfaces can sometimes be perceived as wet or even as a body of water. This is not made easier if someone's sight is diminishing with age. It is also apparent that for some people on the autistic spectrum, some patterns can lead to visually induced cognitive overload or fixation. Migraine, too, can be triggered by high repetitive and contrasting patterns. Careful choice of surface finishes and patterns is therefore an important consideration in any design.

Surface colour

Much is made of colour in some circles, and maybe the jury is still out as to what effect different colours have on our minds and why they have that effect. Even so, some reasonable observations, deductions, hypotheses and outline theories can still be made, providing that precaution is taken when it comes to application.

We know that green and blue appear in abundance in the parts of the world that human populations tend to gravitate to. Where reds and yellows do occur, they tend to make up warm tones that we associate with deciduous woodland, savannas and deserts. However, we tend to associate vibrant reds and yellows with danger. Consequently, you might avoid vibrant reds and yellows in large quantities when designing spaces. Colour wheels can be used to choose what are deemed by some as harmonious and contrasting colours. All this assumes that the user of the design will have sight or eyes that have the capacity to detect colour differences.

However, whilst contrast is good, strongly contrasting tones such as black against white can give rise to what is described by some as scotopic sensitivity, where the eye and brain are thought to find it difficult to process strongly contrasting patterns or text.

It is also thought that some colours may present some people with difficulties. Some think that blue light – with shorter wavelengths than other colours – is easier for our minds to process than red light, which has longer wavelengths. Still others will observe that some have need of a choice of background colour when reading text. Those who have taken an interest in colour include Professor Arnold J. Wilkins[4] and Professor Hillary Dalke.[5] Nevertheless, there is still a lot of debate around the subject.[6] Some of the research is interesting, but it is worth considering whether theories on colour should be applied in too prescriptive a way when it comes to built environments.

CREATIVE COLOUR CAUTION

Perhaps one of the most important things to get across is that whatever the theories are with regard to the effect colours have on people, we are all individuals and the effect of colour will be unique to us all. This is not because the underlying colour theories are not valid but because meaning and metaphor also have significant parts to play. Quite simply, our emotional development will differ and therefore the meaning and metaphor that we associate with different colours will also differ.

When it comes to domestic environments, there is arguably huge freedom for people to choose colours that suit them. However, when it comes to more public or shared environments, caution in the use of colours is advisable. The key thing is to recognize the need for adequate, but not overbearing, tonal contrast between surfaces to enable people to navigate within a space. The next thing is the benefit that colour has in creating a memorable place and creating a mood of a particular place, provided that the colour does not dominate the space. A moderate amount of colour used judicially as a signature in a location that people do not have to look at is advisable. For example, you may want to use some colour in classrooms, not on teaching walls or on the wall that the teacher faces but as a signature colour adjacent to a door. Another example would be a not overbearing but memorable use of colour at junctions in circulation areas. This could help people navigate if used in conjunction with other wayfinding and memory-reinforcing techniques.

Specific surface considerations

Surfaces can have quite far-reaching implications for us, acoustically, thermally and visually, and for how light behaves and how we move. In other words, a lot happens at surfaces. Therefore, the ingredients we use for surfaces in design have profound significance for several of our senses. The worst thing for a designer to do is to specify surfaces on a whim without adequate understanding of how the surfaces they specify interact with diverse human factors. Specify appropriate information, signage and floor, wall and ceiling surface finishes and thereby help people with accentuated neurological needs and visual impairments to identify routes, entrances and other elements and to appreciate the boundaries of spaces without visual stress. As such:

- Apply colours with care, understanding the potential beneficial and negative visual psychological effects of different colours.

  - Aim to develop a thoroughly coordinated and integrated colour pallet from which an appropriate selection can be made for different elements and components in order to enable clarity.

  - Aim for tonal contrasts recommended in guidance. However, avoid using excessive contrast, especially where it is liable to induce confusing and cognitively demanding patterns.

  - Use neutral background tones to achieve tonal contrast, and then use stronger signature colours sparingly in places where they aid place-making but are not 'imposing' themselves on people, especially when people are expected to stay in a particular location for any length of time.

– Avoid relying on colour-based signage and wayfinding information alone, as some people with varying forms of colour blindness will find it difficult to distinguish colours, and people with no sight at all have no use for colour-based information.

• Avoid patterns that make it difficult for some people with accentuated neurological needs to function without sensory overload and make it difficult for some people with visual impairments to see clearly (especially underfoot but also in large wall areas).

– Busy patterns and highly reflective surfaces should be avoided in spaces where visual acuity is critical, such as receptions and speakers' rostrums, as they will hamper communication for people with sensory processing difficulties, impaired vision and those who lip read or use sign language.

– Avoid floor surface finish changes or patterns that could be mistaken for steps or changes of level.

– Avoid highly reflective surfaces that produce glare and cause confusing reflection.

Meanwhile:

• Select surfaces that are conducive to achieving acoustics that are appropriate for the function of the space and the diverse needs of people using the space.

• Choose underfoot surfaces that allow for durability and mobility without excessive effort and without undulation and the risk of slipping, tripping or falling.

• Avoid exposed hot or cold surfaces, especially where these may pose hazards for children and people who may not appreciate the dangers associated with certain surfaces.

20

Tastes, Smells and Air Quality

This chapter identifies the relationship between our minds and our gustatory and olfactory senses.

Tasting one's environment

When an environment is designed, you may think there is little that a person can taste. After all, we do not usually eat our environment. Or do we? If we were to see food growing as part of designing environments, then we do indeed eat our environment. Within some environments the food offer also forms an important experience.

Even if we were not to eat and exercise our gustatory sense directly, the olfactory sense (smell) will often evoke the gustatory sense if there is a food association to be had. Where the smell is not to do with food, a smell may even leave a perception of there being a 'taste in our mouth' that we either like or do not like.

What distinguishes taste from smell is that taste is usually an elective sense (similar to touch) that we choose to deploy for further investigative purposes or enjoyment.

It is common practice within the retail, hospitality, catering and restaurant trades to use aromas to their advantage, not only when it comes to encouraging people to spend money on food but when it comes to enriching the customer experience. In some environments catering for the needs of people with dementia, some organizations purposefully use pleasant food smells to prompt people to eat.[1] For some this will be a pleasurable and joyful experience. However, as the word 'taste' suggests – preferred choice in food and its associated smells will vary to the extent that some will be averse to certain smells. Moreover, for some people, some smells can be difficult to process – as can some tastes. Consequently, in contrast to designing environments with dementia in mind, environments being designed with autism in mind may require careful attention to the avoidance of pervasive aromas.

Whilst some people can be hyper-sensitive to tastes and smells, it should nevertheless be remembered that others are hypo-sensitive and are either unmotivated by tastes and smells or seek them out as they are in need of the sensation to stimulate their brain.

Smelling and breathing in our environment

Although smell and taste are closely related senses, unlike taste, smell is not a particularly elective sense as it cannot be switched on or off without us pinching our nose. Neither is breathing something we have much choice over – especially if we want to stay alive! Consequently, what we smell and breathe in has particular significance to our wellbeing. Like hearing, what we smell and breathe tends to have that residual function to warn us of possible dangers. Not only this, but smell can also evoke memories associated with events that occurred at another time when that smell was sensed.[2]

Some interesting research at Northumbria University under the auspices of Dr Mark Moss, the head of the Department of Psychology, has established that different smells can have an effect on brain function. Whilst there are some rather dubious claims and attributions given to some aromas within some domains, it is interesting nevertheless to note that Northumbria's research found that rosemary enhanced memory and lavender facilitated a sense of calm contentment but hindered memory.[3] Although there seems to be a strong chemical component to this phenomenon, there might also be a sensory processing component to this as well.

Implications for design

If even aromas from herbs have been found to have an effect on the brain, it would not be surprising that general air quality, such as oxygen supply and the presence of other gases or pollutants, is an issue to consider when designing environments. Natural ventilation and air handling systems are particularly important design considerations. Although more difficult to manage, air quality in landscape and urban design is also an important consideration, such as how spaces and routes are arranged in relation to where plants are giving off lots of pollen or where there are vehicle exhaust fumes.

Since smell is not an elective sense, as mentioned, we are very dependent on the nature and design of our environments as to the degree to which we are exposed to smells. Since different materials have different aromas, the choice of building materials will have a bearing on the resulting aroma of an environment. Although this is not necessarily a given, you may reasonably suppose that we would be better adjusted to natural aromas over artificial aromas (apart from the natural aromas that alert us to things that are not pleasant). It is worth thinking about what these might be and whether the environment is one where the consequential aromas are beneficial or not.

Choice within an environment is a key consideration here, and if you were designing an ideal environment, such as an ideal residential, hotel or hospital environment, then you might not leave smell to chance or purposefully use pervasive smells throughout but instead provide options and choices internally that can be switched on, off or between different options. This is arguably more achievable in individual personal spaces such as bedrooms and apartments. However, even where communal spaces, such as large dining rooms and restaurant environments, are being considered, you might provide two or more options between an immersive aromatic environment, a moderately aromatic environment and an environment that is as aromatically neutral as possible. Similarly, in external environments, you might think to use aromatic plants in areas that a person can elect to go to rather than in locations they cannot avoid.

21

Temperature

This chapter identifies the relationship between our minds and our sense of temperature.

Thermal comfort

Some may think of the sensation of temperature as being associated with touch – and indeed it is in part – but it provides us with a different set of information about our environment than the tactile sense (where we determine the texture and topography of a surface). Moreover, temperature is not something that we determine solely by touch. Thus, this chapter focuses on the thermal sense as a distinct sense. Whilst we usually make thermal comfort adjustments through our choice of clothing, the environments that we commission and design also have a significant effect on how comfortable we feel and consequentially how our minds work. If we are not comfortable, we will be distracted. We also know that extreme temperature conditions give rise to conditions such as hypothermia and heat stroke – both of which have very adverse effects on our brain's ability to function!

Some people become susceptible to overheating or becoming too cold and not quite finding the point at which they feel 'just right'. Consequently, they find it difficult to know what the temperature is, in order to make a decision about what clothing to wear, what shelter to find or when to open or close windows in order to remain at the right temperature. This is not helped by some having low blood pressure, poor circulation, paralysis or lack of temperature sensation. We also have different temperature preferences. It becomes apparent that temperature is somewhat influenced not only by how our bodies work but by how we think about temperature.

Air movement

One element of thermal comfort is our ability to detect air movement. Weather forecasts often state that the temperature 'feels' lower when there is wind. We also know that draughts can be particularly uncomfortable.

If temperature differentials within a space are swapped around so that radiant heat from under the floor heats our feet and leaves our heads cooler, then we generally feel more comfortable; whereas if we heat a space so that warmer air rises through convection, our heads get warmer than our feet and we generally feel more uncomfortable. This explains the popularity of underfloor heating.

Perception of temperature is also likely to vary according to whether we are sedentary or moving, near a fire, whether it is sunny or if we are surrounded by blue or red colours. Even so, red does not necessarily make us feel warmer and may make us feel colder due to our own expectations![1] In some highly insulated dwellings that theoretically require no additional heating (other than that gained from our body heat, appliances and the sun) it seems that occupants feel reassured when there are radiators or other heat sources.

Implications for design

Draught reduction, visual access to heat sources, open fires, sunlight and colour schemes all have their psychological benefits indoors. However, the key design consideration is to provide controls and different thermal spaces wherever possible. For example, when it is cold, sheltered sunspots can provide for a sense of wellbeing. Conversely, when it is hot, we seek subterranean spaces, shade and a breeze.

22

The Natural World

This chapter connects sensory integration theory with the theory of biophilia.

The natural world is the context for all forms of sensory stimuli mentioned before.[1] Why is it though that natural environments do not usually give rise to quite the same sensory stresses that some artificial environments give rise to? Why also is it that natural environments appear to benefit us?

Oxygen and temperature

On one hand you could say that most natural, non-urban, low-altitude environments give us access to fresh air capable of supplying sufficient oxygen to keep us alert compared to indoor and urban environments where air quality can be combatively poor. On the other hand, we construct buildings to shelter us from adverse external natural conditions that might lead us to experience brain-numbing hypothermia or heat stroke. So, whilst there is positive potential to be had from natural environments, not all environments that we consider to be natural are good for our minds!

Daylight and views

Many hospitals and office, industrial and retail premises are deep-plan buildings (meaning that many spaces are far from the outside of a building where they could otherwise have windows), and whilst some have views out and an element of daylight can be achieved, the question might be posed – what would the benefits of increased access to daylight, views and natural scenes be?

It has long been suspected that there is a strong correlation between people's wellbeing and their connection with daylight and the outside world. As explained in the chapter on lighting,[2] some people experience the seasonal mood varying effect of reduced natural lighting levels in winter, termed seasonal affective disorder.[3] It has also been discovered that levels of alertness, within the populace in general, are biochemically interconnected with natural daily changes in light colour output.[4]

On occasions when I have visited deep-plan premises, the most notable observation made by employees related to daylight and views out. One member of staff within a deep-plan retail building with no views out expressed how difficult she found having no visual connection with the outside was. Another member of staff in an equivalent building designed with daylight and views expressed how pleasurable it was to work in a building that provided daylight and even commented, 'In how many retail stores could you look out and see sheep?' You can only suppose that such daylight and views significantly improved wellbeing and motivation, not only for staff but also for customers!

Multisensory world

Whilst the visual benefits of the natural environment are arguably the most significant, let us not forget our other senses. It has already been mentioned that physical activity in the external environment benefits a number of senses, including our vestibular and proprioceptive senses.[5] We also know that our chronographic sense (sense of time) benefits from the rhythm of natural light.

What about natural soundscapes? Maybe there is a similar dynamic to the frequency patterns in the visual world? On one hand there are background natural sounds that many of us tend to filter out, whilst we tend to find it harder to filter out sources of certain frequencies or repetitiveness. The sound of a waterfall seems to provide a backdrop, but when water creates a regular drip-drip sound it can even become torturous if we cannot get away from it. In a similar way, the sound of several birds in song often seems pleasurable, but if one is subject to a repetitive, rather tuneless, high-pitched bird call, then one might think differently about the joy of nature!

We also know that many natural environments are the sources of notable and memorable smells. As with artificial smells, we know that whilst some natural smells may be considered pleasurable to some people, some smells are far from pleasurable. Indeed, it is by smell that we know not to eat something that has 'gone off'. Even then, some supposedly pleasurable smells can evoke different responses according to the individual; either because of the different ways we process a smell or because of the emotional or meaning connotations that a smell might have.

Since sound and smell are not easily blocked out, we would do well to create choice of spaces and environments when we commission and design landscapes with regard to sound and smell.

There are also elective senses such as touch (tactile) and taste (gustatory) by which we can enjoy natural environments. However, the caveat to providing tactile and gustatory opportunities is that some individuals on the autistic spectrum can find it difficult to resist the need to seek sensory feedback from certain tastes and tactile sensations. In other words, if there is a choice of external spaces that do not have too much in the way of these stimuli, then this might be considered beneficial for some individuals.

Biophilia

Biophilia, probably means different things to different people, but it could broadly be described as the tendency of people to be drawn to natural environments. People like Bill Browning of Terrapin Bright Green[6] have undertaken work in the area of biophilia and have identified that people recover quicker in hospital where they have access to natural views and that workers with access to a natural outlook are more productive. It is thought that views of natural scenes stimulate the visual senses in a regenerative way. One might therefore see a connection with aspects of sensory processing in which it is known that certain artificial patterns can be difficult for us to process.[7] It is thought that natural patterns have frequencies that tend to cancel one another out (see Figure 22.1), that our minds are better able to filter out natural patterns (so as to identify 'out-of-place' patterns that require our attention) and that we have the freedom to choose whether to engage with natural patterns or not.

Figure 22.1 Natural patterns tend not to cause visual noise

Environmental psychologists have also carried out studies into the relationship between people's wellbeing and their connectivity to the natural environment.[8] The prevalence of blues and greens in the parts of the natural world that we prefer to inhabit may also connect with the ability of our minds to be less stressed in blue and green environments.[9]

People like Dr Mike Wells of Biodiversity by Design[10] have also gone on to emphasize the benefits of people and their habitation being part of a bio-diverse community environment. BREEAM assessments even award credits for views out of buildings in recognition of the reduction on eye strain offered by allowing the eye to periodically refocus on long-distance views.[11] Meanwhile, some lighting manufacturers have even developed bio-dynamic lighting containing programmable colour diodes so as to correlate with circadian rhythms and optimize human productivity.[12]

Biophilic communities?

There is a growing conversation surrounding the benefit of having biophilic cities.[13] However, there is a risk that we objectify biophilia and see nature purely as a biological input that is 'other' than us. We need therefore to constantly remind ourselves that the biosphere is not just about the flora and fauna around us – we are part of the biosphere too! Otherwise, we discover that natural areas within cities become no-go areas after dark. Other than introducing more biodiversity into our built environments, many city parks would be greatly improved if they were to include dwellings that enabled stewardship roles and fostered both greater biodiversity and human enjoyment of our parks at the same time.

Biomimicry

Product manufactures are introducing biomimicry in to their products – particularly flooring products such as carpets. However, when walking across even surfaces, our brains may struggle to adjust to biomimicry if it is used in locations where we might not expect it – because we use different schemas (subconscious 'programmes') for different situations.

Implications for design

We should be designing new environments where access to natural environments is more purposeful. However, when it comes to existing environments, I would suggest owners of deep-plan buildings commission a survey of their staff and customers to elicit what, to them, are significant environmental factors affecting their wellbeing at work. Surveys could also be used to collate other data of benefit to a business when considering staff wellbeing, customer experience and store design. Such a study should not focus on lighting, views and access to the natural world alone, as this could give rise to prompting answers to closed questions. With these survey results, a range of pilot projects could be put into effect as and when opportunities present themselves to apply knowledge gained from engagement and research.

When it comes to designing schools for children and students on the autistic spectrum, however, it is just as important to have manageable choice regarding views out and this can enable focus, avoid distraction, reduce sensory overload and improve perceived behaviour. However, it should be recognized that access to daylight and the opportunity to find visual relief are important means of reducing sensory overload and distraction. The key is the means to managing choice.

What could the results of improvements be?

When it comes to mainstream environments, we would anticipate an increased sense of staff wellbeing, motivation, retention, loyalty and productivity through greater alertness and reduced risk of downward shifts in mood and mental health. It could also be concluded that features which benefit staff could, in retail and service environments, be identified as improving the customer and service user experience, either directly as a result of daylight and views or indirectly as a result of happier staff. Implementation of changes could also further any corporate community and social responsibility agendas.

23

Time and Memory

This chapter connects space, time and memory.

Time

How we orientate ourselves in time is significantly affected by our ability to track changes in our environment on a daily basis. Whilst seasonal changes will help augment our ability to track the progress of time over the course of a year, the effect that light has on our daily circadian rhythm also helps our brains regulate our sense of time on a shorter-term basis.[1] The ability of us all to function effectively depends not only on the opportunity to keep track of external changes, but on whether the artificial light that we are subjected to works with or against our circadian rhythm. People with Parkinson's disease or attention or hyperactivity difficulties are also thought to have greater difficulties in relation to tracking time due to how parts of their brain function.[2]

Memory

When it comes to memory, keeping track of time is no doubt a key factor. We have also noted that some aromas appear to have an effect on our memory.[3] However, the role that context has on our ability to remember things is particularly significant.

When you are undertaking a task in one room and need something to complete that task in another room, how many times have you forgotten why you went there? When you go to the other room, how often do retrace your steps and recapture the memory in the original room? It is almost as if doors are 'memory portals' that wipe your memory when you leave a space.[4] When we re-enter a space, the context helps us to remember the thought processes we had there.

From my experience, people with dyslexia (and similar neurological experiences relating to the processing of information) often struggle with working memory[5] and so will tend to place extra reliance on spatial memory in familiar visual environments they have control over as their aide-mémoire when it comes to revisiting tasks in their workplace. Consequently, workplace designs that are totally dependent on hot-desking and clear-desk policies place people with dyslexia and other memory-related neurological conditions at a disadvantage. To remove these aide-mémoires could be likened to kicking a walking aid out from underneath someone!

People living with dementia usually maintain long-term and visceral memory for longer; these are memories that are more easily accessed by emotions compared to short-term memory, for which factual recall is harder.[6] Moreover, in familiar environments, we all develop schemas (subconscious, 'automated' processes) in which we need to think little about what we are doing. Consequently, maintaining familiar environments for people living with dementia or other memory loss experiences is particularly important – in order to help maintain their independence for as long as possible. Otherwise, removing people from familiar environments can lead to a significant decline in someone's functioning memory and independence. In order to mitigate this decline in independence when relocation is unavoidable, moving familiar objects and furnishings to the new location can help people recall memories. Pictures of local landmarks taken when the person was younger will also help them to recall memories. A note of caution, though: some individuals may recall stress and trauma when pictures and environments replicate scenes that they associate with trauma.

Implications for design

We do not operate in isolation to context. Without context we have nothing to interact with, neither physiologically nor neurologically. It is not surprising, therefore, that how we design and manage the environments and the context to our lives will have an impact on how our memory works and how we keep track of time. The implications of time and memory for design could be seen as falling into several areas:

- Providing access to daylight and views will help people to keep track of time.

- Providing control of light sources at night will help some people (particularly those living with dementia) to sleep without waking prematurely.

- Creating memorable spaces (place-making) on circulation routes will help people recall where they are when it comes to wayfinding.

- Providing and managing workplace environments that support people's working memory, without insisting on mandatory hot-desk and clear-desk policies, will help people function better – especially when they use stronger spatial memory to compensate for working memory difficulties.

- Maintaining familiar environments with familiar objects helps people living with dementia to maintain independence.

- Replicating familiar environments may help some people living with dementia if they have had to move.

- You might want to avoid using copious amounts of lavender[7] in either landscapes close to buildings or as an air freshener if you want people to be productive or where individuals are already struggling to be alert or remember things (such as in schools or in environments serving people living with dementia). Rosemary as an aroma might help people function at their best, provided that it is not imposed as an aroma.[8]

24

Navigation, Place and Wayfinding

This chapter identifies the significance of place-making, orientation and wayfinding.

Different users of an environment should be able to find their way from a point of arrival within an environment, via an accessible route, to their destination. A sense of place, wayfinding and orientation make this possible, but these are hugely dependent on sensory clues and the different ways that people process and integrate sensory information.

Wayfinding

Wayfinding is about access to clues that assist us whilst navigating environments. It includes providing clues as to place and orientation, including:

- memorability and familiarity of place

- architectural clarity (i.e., logical arrangements and clear identification of place, routes, entrances and elements)

- visual and cognitive clarity in terms of tonal contrast between building elements without causing visual noise

- good lighting that avoids discomfort and confusion by avoiding excessive reflections, glare and shadowing

- supporting signage and symbols

- external tactile hazard identification and route information

- acoustics that lead to clear interpretation of sound and speech when asking for assistance.

Whether an environment is an individual building or an external urban environment, people should be able to identify entrances, places of reception and key facilities – particularly parking, toilets, stairs, lifts and significant/principal destinations in an environment. It is particularly beneficial if place-making techniques are used to distinguish between otherwise easily confused locations, distinguishing floor levels and stairs and confirming arrival at destinations.

Welcome and convenience

Feeling that one is welcome and can ask for help is often essential to an inclusive experience. Consequently, good first impressions and effective early communication[1] are crucial. Points of reception are key, as these are places where one might expect to receive assistance and from where managers are able to implement management strategies to assist. Even so, it is attitude that really makes the difference. With good attitudes in place, you can support good human-centric design.

Another key factor is ease of getting to and from toilets. The more obvious and apparent the locations of toilets are, the more convenient they will be! This reduces stress arising from circumstances where individuals urgently need to find a toilet, or where neurological needs such as dementia are such that visual prompters regarding the availability of toilets reduce the likelihood of mishaps occurring, and clarity of exit routes decreases the risk of distress.[2]

Signage

It is all too easy for wayfinding to be equated solely with signage. Wayfinding should not be only reliant on signage, but signage should support wayfinding. It should assist people, not only those with sight loss or no sight but also people with neurological and language needs, whilst they navigate environments.

Do not be fooled by the notion that buildings 'speak for themselves' and the opinion that any use of signage is an admission of a design's failure. Yes, signage can be used as a 'sticking plaster', but even in well-designed environments it is often necessary to provide supplementary assistance in the form of signage. Signage is therefore part of wayfinding, but not the *entirety* of wayfinding.

Signage should be well planned and an integrated part of the wider principles of wayfinding. It should be located where directional choices need to be made or other information needs to be conveyed, such as informing users of particular routes and what they might expect if they use a particular route – e.g., steps or ramps. It should be used on return routes as well as arrival routes and identify which routes are accessible to people with mobility difficulties. Signage should also support the wayfinding of people with specific sensory and neurological needs whilst navigating environments. It comes in four principal types:

- directory – provision of a choice of destinations

- direction – establishment of route through access sequence

- destination/identification – confirmation of arrival/identity of a place

- information – safety/regulatory/fire/instruction.

Signage should be clear, logical and succinct; easily understood; and only used when necessary. It should maximize the visibility and legibility of information, and it should use recognized symbols, plain language, easy-to-read typefaces/fonts, lower case, sentence case or title case text and sufficient tonal contrast between text and background. It is also helpful if the contrast between text and background is not too stark. This is because some people find that jet black text on a stark white background is difficult to read, process and decipher.

Upper case text takes longer to read and is more difficult for people with dyslexia. The benefit of using lower case, sentence case or title case text on signage is that it enables people to more easily read whole words by recognizing their outline and shape, whereas when text is written in capitals people usually have to decipher the meaning of a word by assembling the individual letters first.

The design of signage should consider the distance from which the information is being read; be consistent, using recommended heights, locations, sizes, typefaces, colours and contrast found in the *Sign Design Guide*.[3]

Multisensory needs

Wayfinding and signage (in terms of routes and information) design needs take into account the needs of people with visual, hearing and neurological impairments as well as the mobility/stamina/dexterity of users; warn or steer people from hazards; and lead people to a place of safety in an emergency.

Let us not forget that people with visual and hearing impairments also have a neurological need for understanding the environment around them. Unless information is available in a form that they can decipher, they will find it harder to function in that environment not only on a visual level but on a cognitive and participative level. If you feel isolated, you will feel neurologically disadvantaged, as you will have not benefitted from the information and participation that others take for granted. From the perspective of particular sensory needs, it is therefore important to consider the following range of means of communication:

- tactile and braille signage where there are logical locations for the signage and where braille can be located easily

- duplicating signage information at different reading heights where, in certain situations, one height may make it difficult to read signage

- tactile and braille maps (that are not overly complicated) where there are logical locations and where maps can be located easily

- tag 'signs' (proximity triggered audible output via smart phone or radio devices)

- GPS systems (similar to car-based satellite navigation systems – but they relay more detailed information audibly)

- sign language interpretation of visual, printed and auditory information

- captioning of auditory information

- acoustic and visually distinguishable places that help location.

In addition to the Sign Design Guide, the UK's NHS Estates publication *Wayfinding*[4] is a particularly useful document.

Pre- and on-arrival information

Pre-arrival information via printed information and web pages (designed to web access standards) are often crucial and best made available in different formats such as large text, foreign language text, Makaton[5] supported text, braille, audio tape/CD and/or electronic files. This is because people who anticipate difficulties navigating and manoeuvring around an environment often like to prepare themselves as much as possible. This is no less relevant to some people with accentuated neurological needs than it is relevant to people with mobility, visual and auditory needs.

On-arrival information in different formats is also important and best managed at a point of reception. However, some notice boards can give rise to sensory and cognitive overload, particularly in otherwise busy entrances. Consequently, information signage could also be a means of framing and regulating temporary notice board-type information displays, in order that it is sufficient but not too much for the intended purpose of communication. Such information displays need to be easily updated, be maintained and be well lit but avoid excessive reflection, glare and shadowing that would otherwise hinder reading.

Symbols

Historically, standardized public information symbols (such as British Standards Institution (BSI) and International Organization for Standardization (ISO) symbols) have been developed principally for transport, sports and leisure environments. This could be largely due to the international dimension of these activities, which demands recognizable symbols as a means by which people can find their way around irrespective of language.

The significance of symbols to wayfinding (in addition to spatial, visual, graphical and tactile clarity) is that they help communicate where words alone may not. If a person with learning difficulty uses symbols and signing (such as Makaton symbols and signing) as an essential part of their daily communication, then they may be further enabled if they see and understand symbols used in the wider community. They can also help children, speakers of other languages and the population as a whole.

Although variant forms of symbol typology can be seen as desirable, there is always the risk that they might become unintelligible to people, especially those reliant on strong linguistic consistency or what I would call a consistent 'code'. Within industrial and workplace environments, where symbols relate predominantly to safety, they have tended to be highly standardized. Symbols developed for retail environments, on the other hand, tend to be less standardized and more dependent on branding trends. However, retail environments would do well to avoid being too 'clever' and use symbols that most people would understand.

It is, however, within education, civic and healthcare environments that it would make particular sense to further progress the use of symbols through the availability of a more comprehensive 'vocabulary' of standardized symbols, which are currently lacking in these environments.

Specialist and standard symbols

The extent to which specialist text-support symbols such as Makaton symbols might themselves be used on signage is debatable. It is worth pointing out that Makaton has been developed more around text and language support than wayfinding use. In other words, whilst Makaton is a disciplined symbol system, it has not been designed to be viewed at a distance and to be viewed on its own.

In certain environments, you might advocate the use of Makaton symbols on signage itself as a means of confirming interpretation by Makaton users encountering standard public information symbols for the first time. This might be particularly important in environments where higher levels of Makaton usage are anticipated, such as in educational environments.

In more public realms, though, standardized wayfinding symbols such as BSI and ISO symbols are likely to be more beneficial, and so Makaton could potentially be used as a 'subtext' dependent on closer inspection, in a similar way to braille, so as to encourage primary reliance on the more iconic BSI and ISO symbols.

Enabling information

As a means to reinforcing wayfinding, managers of any publicly accessed environments should be encouraged to also provide explanatory and translated information to Makaton users on arrival to environments, including explanation of any BSI symbols used. Website information with Makaton translation could also provide support workers with resources with which to prepare Makaton users prior to visiting an environment. However, it is most important to consult the Makaton Charity before undertaking any such translation exercise in order to achieve meaningful and appropriate outcomes.

My hope is to see an increased lexicon of standard public information symbols and to establish the equivalent of the Rosetta Stone, enabling Makaton and other symbol users to learn and understand the equivalent BSI and ISO symbols for the environments they seek to navigate. Arguably, standardized wayfinding symbols ought to be seen on signage alongside braille, tonal contrast and tactile text as means of assisting people with differing requirements while wayfinding within environments.

Points to note

When designing, it is worth avoiding the design of:

- architectural duality, where there are unnecessary and unexplained choices provided to no advantage

- wayfinding and/or signage that inadvertently leads people into danger

- reflective signage surfaces where veiling reflections inhibit the reading of any wayfinding information

- visually 'busy' environments, which detract from the clear distinctions between elements and lead to sensory and neurological overload

- visually bland environments, which lack distinction between zones or departments

- acoustic environments that inhibit communication where communication is expected

- notices that get stuck up in an uncoordinated and counterproductive manner or stuck on doors, causing visual obstructions

- text that incorporates jargon or abbreviations, upper case text and/or intricate or abstract fonts/typefaces

- superfluous wayfinding information, such as 'Department' following the description of the department

- dead-end circulation routes within care settings where there are people living with dementia who might find it difficult to work out their next move

- mirrors at the end of circulation routes that give the appearance of someone obstructing a person's way within care settings where there are people living with dementia, who might not recognize themselves or the presence of a mirror.

25

Spatial Choice, Permission and Security

This chapter sets out the importance of choice, the pros and cons of perceived permissions and the effect that spatial configuration can have on how we feel.

If you remember nothing else from this book (other than the significance of sensory processing and context-based memory), it is worth remembering the importance of choice *and* permission.

Choice

People will seek out different stimuli within either a spatial or a social context, according to their own sensory needs at any particular time. Whilst we cannot design every space to suite everybody, we can usually employ design strategies to create calm environments in general together with a range of particularly well-placed stimuli. For example, spaces that we create within new or renewed environments could provide different opportunities for varying degrees of social interaction, solitary activity, sleep, rest, work, exercise, reflection, etc. No one space can provide for all of these activities at once where other people are around. However, we can provide alternative spaces. It might also be argued that the root cause of boredom is the lack of sensory exercise and alternatives. Without a choice of opportunity and sensory exercise, boredom and cabin fever could arise. Whether or not there is one or more person involved, choice of sensory environments is still necessary.

Security

In architecture, we usually utilize the notion of 'defensible' space combined with 'natural surveillance' to define implied territory. This is where those entering an environment are likely to consider that someone *could* be watching them, either giving them a sense of personal security (if their reason for being there is genuine) or, if they are planning something untoward, dissuading them from their course of action. Such defensible space is often signalled by curtilages and/or intermediate 'threshold' spaces such as cul-de-sac roads, front gardens or the presence of 'portal' features such as gateways and doorways (see Figure 25.1). You can see this principle in how spaces are sequentially configured in castles (see Figure 25.2).

Figure 25.1 Thresholds convey privacy and dissuade uninvited entry

Figure 25.2 Defensible space does not always need to be clearly defined

A sense of natural surveillance is often conveyed by actual human activity or by inferred human presence through the provision of windows or other vantage points facing onto the environment in question. Indeed, we tend to perceive windows as 'eyes' from which the potential surveillance occurs. Consequently, other than the presence of physical barriers, security often depends on whether people *perceive* that they have permission to enter an environment and, when they do enter that environment, whether they feel welcome. This is not so much because someone has told a person anything but because the way an environment is set out communicates in the built-environment equivalent of body language. We might describe this as the physical language of territoriality.

Where an urban environment has a lack of windows looking onto it, social 'blind' spots occur and we might see the signs of antisocial behaviour in the form of graffiti or fly tipping occurring. In such environments we can often feel uneasy (see Figure 25.3). Another principle of natural surveillance is the sense of security in numbers, so where there are more people in an external space than usual, people will usually feel more secure, even if that is in locations where most other people are in vehicles. Consequently, infrequently accessed pedestrian spaces often feel more insecure.

Figure 25.3 Spaces without windows make us feel insecure

The lack of perceived territoriality in some environments can be a significant problem, especially in housing. This can usually be found where private space is too near to public space and where there is a lack of transition between the two. Moreover, if there is ambiguity over the right to be within transitional space, this can also cause problems. This tends to be the situation where communal circulation areas provide access to large numbers of people but where a person does not feel able to 'challenge' others who may have no valid reason for being there. The general wisdom in communal housing is to limit shared access to a small number of apartments at one time, since a person is more likely to feel that they have the 'right to challenge' anyone within that communal environment.

Given the choice, most people feel most relaxed and secure if they are able to find a location from which they have the sense of refuge, prospect and opportunity to escape. This means being able to achieve your own natural surveillance and defensible space – without the fear that someone might come up behind you. Seating shielded from behind, with a view over landscape, is one of the most relaxing spaces you can find yourself in (see Figure 25.4). Likewise, if you have the opportunity to choose a seat in a restaurant and find a table where you can sit against a wall and look towards the main entrance and out of the restaurant, then you are likely to feel more relaxed (see Figure 25.5). However, the sense of prospect is not just about being able to maintain your own natural surveillance; it is also about the opportunity for sensory stimulation through being able to see what is happening beyond your immediate surroundings.

Figure 25.4 Refuge – seating shielded from behind

Figure 25.5 Prospect – view from a vantage point

Permission

Arguably, you want people in some environments to feel comfortable enough to do what you want them to do and not feel inhibited. There are particular environments, especially where people are likely to spend a large amount of time, where a perceived lack of permission to do what you want them to do can be a significant problem. These include:

- work environments

- hospital, health and social care environments

- some exhibition environments

- some custodial environments.

Workplaces

Dr Craig Knight, the occupational psychologist noted earlier in the book, has undertaken research along with Professor Alex Haslam into what the effects of choice and permission are in workplaces.[1] They have identified that people who work in 'empowered' workplaces, where there is choice and permission to adapt their own environment, are more productive than those in 'enriched' workplaces, where their employers have created the stimuli. Those in 'enriched' workplaces are in turn more productive than those who work in 'lean' workplaces, where there is a distinct lack of stimulus or permission to adapt one's workplace. Finally, they found that if a person has an 'empowered' workplace and then choice and permission are removed, the performance of workers in what would then be a 'disempowered' workplace plummets!

Some would argue for activity-based workplaces and choice of environment, and yes, this is good; but it does not fully respond to the significance of a person having permission to create an environment conducive to them. We have already noted[2] that where autism, dyslexia and other diverse neurological experiences are concerned, this becomes even more poignant, as the greater a person's ability to control their environment and the greater the reassurance of predictability, the greater scope they have to manage their sensory stress levels and to support their memory. These workplaces could be referred to as individually controllable spaces or work nests (see Figure 25.6).

Figure 25.6 A random workplace nest

Hospital, health and social care

It is all too easy for people within hospital, health and social care settings to feel that they lack a sense of permission to do things for themselves that aid their wellbeing. Some of this lack of permission can be portrayed through how environments are designed and the image that they present. If people are expected to be in an environment for any length of time, the more homely an environment feels, the greater the likelihood that person will feel they have permission to do that which is conducive to their wellbeing.

Exhibitions

Alastair Somerville of Acuity Design,[3] in his information design work, often identifies that the lack of perceived permission to stop in exhibition environments can lead to a sense of information and cognitive overload if there is little opportunity for people to rest on a journey through the exhibition. This can be even more acute if exhibition designers are so intent on providing visitors with an intense and unforgettable multisensory experience that they forget to provide opportunity and a sense of permission to recuperate and reflect!

Custodial environments

Whilst the removal of permission is an explicit feature of custodial environments, there is nevertheless a question to be posed that relates to rehabilitation and enabling offenders to re-enter society. Arguably, the more that a person is provided with the opportunity to engage in positive and self-directed activity, the less likely they are to become institutionalized or to leave expecting that society owes them something. The positive design of custodial environments could therefore do much to offer incentives through a sense of appropriate permission.[4]

26

Communication

A key objective of many environments is the transmission, reception and understanding of information, in which speech, hearing, sight and neurological processes play a major part, especially where people have additional neurological, hearing and visual needs.

One of the most neurologically intense activities that we engage in is communication. Not only are there significant sensory aspects to communication, but communication requires a considerable amount of neurological activity, including memory, to decipher what others are saying and to formulate a response. Consequently, the design of environments is a significant consideration.

Getting the acoustics and lighting right is a prerequisite to good communication within an environment. However, in this age of information technology, we need to remember the emergence of another realm of 'architecture': information architecture. Getting the design of pre-arrival and on-arrival information right, whether in digital, printed, braille, audio-visual or personal communication terms, means that we are engaging more in designing services for which the physical architecture forms an important context and potential enabler.

So significant is communication that various aspects of the subject are covered in some depth in other chapters as well.[1]

Different Environments

This section discusses enabling particular types of mind-friendly environment.

27

Landscape and Urban

If nothing else, landscapes and urban realms are the wider external context in which our minds operate and in which every other environment is to be found.

Context

Landscapes and urban realms provide the 'backdrop' beyond or behind what we do. We know from previous chapters that such contexts provide us with the sensory ingredients that our minds need in order to operate effectively.[1] We also know that our memory – i.e., recollections – are significantly influenced by the context in which a thought occurred.[2]

Multiple stimuli

Stimuli in external environments are usually quite extensive and varied. In general, the natural environment consists of visual stimuli, which our brains usually cope with better than visual stimuli in artificial environments.[3] However, auditory, olfactory or underfoot, tactile stimuli are not usually elective. So whilst natural environments give rise to sensory stimuli that are usually beneficial, some can give rise to pervasive stimuli we can find problematic (such as repetitive, tuneless bird calls or pungent plant aromas that some individuals find unpleasant). The key thing to remember therefore is choice and opportunities for finding calm through to intense stimulus. The aim should be to avoid imposing intense sensory stimuli where they cannot be avoided but also providing opportunities for finding sensory stimulus where one has choice to be stimulated or not.

Navigation

A key ingredient in landscape and urban environments is orientation – both spatially and in time. In other words, orientation is not just about wayfinding but recollection, too. Whilst signage is helpful,[4] it helps in landscape and urban environments if there is sensory variety – in other words, virtual 'topography' within each sensory domain, through which we can distinguish one place from another and by which our memories might be stimulated to recollect. This is usually referred to as the act of place-making.

Security

Whereas most built environments afford us a sense of security because we are enclosed by walls, landscape and urban realms do not always provide enclosure. In certain instances, a sense of enclosure might be a valuable design aim. However, a sense of security can also be achieved where the design provides the perception that others are around through the presence of habitation, activity, passing traffic and overlooking windows.[5]

Design opportunities

Dr Katie Gaudion and Chris McGinley have published *Green Spaces: Outdoor Environments for Adults with Autism*, which provides some valuable insights.[6] Meanwhile, whilst bearing in mind the importance of choice, orientation/wayfinding and security, there are many design opportunities that landscape and urban environments are capable of providing and that can be explored when we consider people's diverse neurological needs and sensory inputs. There are opportunities to:

- introduce natural scenes, which bring great benefit if introduced into urban environments, whilst avoiding problematic patterns[7]

- design ways by which daylight, sunlight, shade and shadow can be managed in order to achieve visually uplifting and sensory calm spaces[8]

- Work with aromas, taste and other senses where there is fruit picking, gardening and/or food outlets

- Introduce stimulating textures that offer an opportunity for touch,[9] both in terms of planting and hard landscape

- utilize water and other features to stimulate auditory senses[10] (see Figure 27.1)

- exercise vestibular and proprioceptive senses, not only through enabling movement (via walking, assistive mobility or cycling) but in sport or play through sport facilities, obstacles and playground design[11]

- foster thermal comfort, whether it be the creation of sun traps and other micro-climates or by providing shelter from a cold wind or a hot sun.[12]

As such, before seeking to commission or design landscapes and urban environments, you would be best advised to consult someone with the necessary mind-friendly knowledge.

Figure 27.1 Utilizing water to stimulate auditory senses

28

Transport

If nothing else, transport environments are about transition from one place to another and are therefore about a change of the context in which our minds operate.

Transition

Transport and the act of transition from one place to another can bring about either refreshing stimulation or stress. Visual changes in scenery can be beneficial as we travel, but constant change and complexity might also lead to sensory overload to varying degrees amidst the population as a whole. Furthermore, when we travel, we are subject to:

- constant noise and occasional smells that we cannot escape from and temperatures that we have little or no control of

- impositions on our body clocks that we have to recover from

- restrictions on our tactile, vestibular and proprioceptive comfort/activity

- anxieties associated with preparing for, waiting and getting transport connections.

It is not surprising, therefore, that the sensory challenges associated with transport often mean that people can easily become stressed and confused in transport environments.

Quiet spaces

It is not uncommon for there to be little choice of environment either on modes of transport themselves or at transport interconnections, unless you have the money to pay. However, the provision of mind-friendly waiting areas would transform many transport environments into more inclusive places, particularly for people living with dementia or on the autistic spectrum. Quiet, comfortable options with alternative places for activity and exercise are options that could improve many transport environments.

Informative environments

Legible and informative environments, in which a person can orientate themselves, find their connection and know what is expected of them are crucial to the transport experience. Wayfinding is important, but it needs to be understood in the round and as part of a much wider information environment, also considering the modes of communication and different formats of information that different people need, such as braille, sign language, plain language and text support symbols or illustrations. In other words, good transport environments are not just about transition but about transfer of information as well. Consequently, when designing transport environments, you need to understand not only the passenger experience (customer journey) within the built environment but the passenger experience within the information environment as well.[1]

Design criteria and opportunities

There are many design criteria that ought to be explored when we consider people's diverse neurological needs within transport environments:

- stress-reductive acoustics[2]

- visual relief in the form of views of natural environments[3]

- alternative, quiet waiting areas in which a person can rest their senses

- activity space design in which a person can exercise their senses[4]

- wayfinding design by which a person can navigate to, from and between connections[5]

- place-making by which a person can recollect where they are in relation to other locations within and beyond the transport environment

- inclusive information design/architecture by which a person can comprehend what is expected and how to make their connections.[6]

However, before seeking to commission or design transport environments, you would be best advised to consult someone with mind-friendly knowledge.

29

Education

If nothing else, education environments are about the transfer of information from one mind to another.

Transfer of information

The process of education, perhaps more than any other, exemplifies the importance of understanding the relationship between our minds and the environment around us. The transfer of information involved in education entails a significant amount of sensory processing, which is reflected in different learning styles such as multisensory, visual, auditory, kinaesthetic (tactile, vestibular and proprioceptive), reflective, individual-working and group-working styles.

Diverse learning styles

Yes, transfer of information is important, but so too is the transfer of understanding and enthusiasm. The more people's different senses are engaged, the more likely these transfers will be enabled to take place. In order for this to happen, the learning environment needs to be conducive to the sensory needs of its users. You could perhaps suppose that:

- those who fidget need to exercise their tactile, vestibular and proprioceptive senses to engage in learning effectively, because they are more kinaesthetic in their learning

- those who doodle need to exercise their visual senses in order to learn

- those who need music on in the background are more auditory learners.

Some students on the other hand will find it difficult to concentrate in the learning process if they are subject to auditory, visual or other sensory distractions. When undertaking one-to-one studio tutoring at one school of architecture, I discovered that a number of students found that the bold, regular pattern at each end of the studio was visually noisy and made them feel dizzy. There was also little positive visual relief in the form of views out.

What is apparent is that in order to learn, different people have different needs, not all of which can be met at the same time when a group is being taught by a teacher from the front. You can get some basic things right by reducing distractions for those that find distractions difficult and providing the right amount of stimulus. The next thing you can do is provide opportunities for people to find the spaces that are conducive to individual or group learning. Then there is the selection of furniture that enables tactile, vestibular and proprioceptive exercise and/or support. You might also suggest that opportunities for activities such as music, art, woodwork, metalwork, sports, drama, play and food provide pupils/ students opportunities to exercise their senses in between more sedentary learning.

Design criteria and opportunities

Opportunities for the design of positive learning environments include:

- a range of furniture conducive to both comfort and exercise of vestibular and proprioceptive senses, including rocking classroom chairs[1]

- a calm acoustic design that enables noise reduction and reverberation times suitable to learning, with reduced reverberation times where individuals are known to have additional learning or hearing needs[2]

- visual environments that avoid distractions, patterns or colours on the teaching wall or opposite the teaching wall but allow opportunity for moderate visual stimulus when conducive to the learning process and those being taught[3]

- opportunities for views out over natural scenery whilst also providing the opportunity to control views, levels of sunlight and levels of daylight according to the situation and those being taught[4]

- well-designed and controlled natural and artificial lighting, designed according to the situation and those being taught[5]

- a range of spaces conducive to individual and group learning with access to views out where possible

- play, performance and sport spaces indoors and externally

- creative spaces indoors and externally

- food production, preparation and consumption spaces.

Much of the above you would expect to find in an educational environment, but designing these spaces with an understanding of neurological benefits could significantly influence the approach that you take. Therefore, before seeking to commission or design education environments, you would be best advised to consult someone with insightful mind-friendly knowledge.

30

Health and Social Care

If nothing else, health and social care should be not only about physical wellbeing but about wellbeing of the mind too.

Wellbeing or stress?

Perhaps more than any other environment, other than education, health and social care environments ought to be where the relationship between our minds and our environments should to be understood. However, it is all too easy to find challenging health and social care environments. Rather than experiencing wellbeing, many a person can experience sensory overload in these environments.

The design of healthcare environments has often been driven by hygiene requirements, functional lighting levels and basic medical efficiencies, with little attention to calming acoustics and relaxing visuals. Many hospitals have rooms that have no views owing to deep plans; highly reverberant spaces owing to hard, washable surfaces; and intense, bright artificial light with a lack of adjustment in level or colour output. Some social care environments may be better, yet it is not uncommon to find either overtly clinical environments or old and visual confusing environments with problematic carpet patterns.

A classic example of where problems have occurred is in premature baby units, where babies have suffered as a result of the very clinical environment that they were in.[1] The concern is that intense lighting, noise from equipment, alarms, reverberant surfaces, things being stuck to their skin and the potential for intense smells has led to children experiencing sensory overload and developing sensory hyper-sensitivity. Moreover, detachment from parents whilst on hospital wards during early development means that they miss out on important the sensory reassurance that comes from being held.

I am also aware of a scenario in which patients were being admitted onto a psychiatric ward, and a clinician suspected that the degree of sensory overload was so counterproductive that patients were getting worse and not better as a result. Therefore, this is a subject that warrants urgent research to substantiate (or otherwise) this suspected causal link.

Realizing that some hospital environments appear very clinical, some designers have taken to visual enhancements, especially in children's hospitals. In some hospitals, the effect is sensory overload with intense colours and lots of visual designs going on both floors and walls. There are also instances of healthcare environments where the assumption has been that just by employing well-known architects, the flagship architecture of these professionals will 'magically' work wonders on people's minds. Whilst it is apparent that some of these architects have indeed come up with uplifting designs, it is also apparent that some lack an understanding of what makes for inclusive and mind-friendly design.

If environmental issues were not enough, it is all too easy to find hospitals where the wayfinding leaves a lot to be desired, and where the stress of not easily finding their way prior to an appointment is not really what a patient wants to experience.

Health and social care workers

We may also be tempted to think only from the perspective of someone receiving health or social care and neglect to think about those working in such environments. If environments are more conducive to the minds of those who work in them, then it stands to reason that they will be better able to support those who seek help. Where staff are responsible for vulnerable individuals, it benefits them too if these individuals can be calm and free from stress and if staff are able to remain accountable for their whereabouts without the risk of either overbearing supervision or individuals wandering off and coming to harm.[2]

One particularly interesting study assessed the difference, for both staff and patients, between open-plan wards and individual rooms for patients.[3] On one hand, you can understand the argument for individual rooms in controlling infection, reducing sensory intrusion and increasing privacy, but this gave rise to anxiety amongst staff. Staff were finding it difficult to maintain an overview of their patients' needs and found it difficult to work collectively, and patients were unable to see what was going on in order to understand staff workloads and priorities. Dividing the beds between rooms interfered with the natural benefits afforded by peripheral pre-conscious awareness that enables those undertaking focused tasks to maintain awareness of changes going on around them before they become critical. Perhaps the issues could be balanced more effectively if designers understood not only sensory processing but also the significance of how certain activities such as nursing necessitate the use of our brain's potential to maintain both focused and peripheral attention.

Design criteria and opportunities

Whilst there are a few criteria and opportunities for the design of health and social care environments, when it comes to designing such environments, it is worth reading this book through from cover to cover to consider all the ideas presented. Nevertheless, what you are looking to achieve is:

- attenuation of sensory noise and opportunities for sensory relief and change[4]

- ways of creating sensory calm environments, good visual access to views and daylight[5]

- familiarization with safeguarding of wellbeing considerations[6]

- activities for all users of an environment to exercise their senses in a restorative way

- opportunities by which the environment will help facilitate group therapy and therapeutic activity, such as talking, music, art and sports therapy as well as opportunities for individuals to find personal space too.

You may have heard of the term psychologically informed environments. There are various websites that explain what this is about. It seems mainly to revolve around informing practice around working with homeless people through gathering psychological insights. Although, it is not so much about physical environments, it could also give rise to interesting insights, not only to the field of working with homeless people but other people within health and social care settings. Nevertheless, before seeking to commission or design health and social care environments, you would be best advised to consult someone with applicable mind-friendly knowledge.

31

Workplaces

If nothing else, workplace, commercial, civic and business environments are about productivity and service.

Productivity

The workplace is the context in which we expect people and their minds to function – but are we taking account of the impact that the sensory environment has on people's minds?

It is not uncommon to find workplace design decisions that resolve around simplistic imagery and cost savings. Could we better inform the design process by a greater awareness of the user experience? How many employees or customers are stressed or at risk of leaving the journey that businesses are taking them on? Many a workplace design sales pitch includes words like 'trendy' or 'value engineered', but are we actually removing real, lasting value – derived from how people experience the business environments that are designed and operated? These pitches might even reference terms such as 'lean', 'agile', 'smart' or 'activity-based' workplace strategies. But are we creating an illusion?

How about stepping back from these trendy terms for a moment and paying attention to what your senses (and the senses of those around you) are telling you. What could our senses be telling us about our work environments? We know that much of that which takes place as a consequence of our senses is not in the realm of our sensory organs but in how our brains function whilst processing sensory information. How effectively do our brains function, then, if our senses are struggling with the environment that we find ourselves within?

We could be taking the opportunity to step back and spend time in the workplaces we design or that our employees or customers are using. We may already be one of those 'captains of industry' who work amongst your staff. Is the sensory experience around us conducive to us doing effective work? Maybe you cope, at least for a time...but how about others? Are we all the same? How about those who tirelessly work on thankless tasks requiring great concentration but are stressed out by the environment they are working in? Chances are we will find out a lot just by talking to colleagues. We might find it a struggle understand their sensory experiences because we may have managed our own sensory needs subconsciously without stopping to think what is happening. As such, it might even help if we listen to individuals with accentuated experiences in order to better understand our own needs.

Design opportunities

We can deduct from what we know of sensory and physiological needs that:

- interactive, adjustable and comfortable chairs and tables are necessary if we are to expect workers to function fully[1]

- optimized acoustics are essential to avoid distraction and reduce stress[2]

- good background lighting and good task lighting are also important, but so too is natural light and access to views of nature.[3]

But what else is there that we could be doing? For example, could we being taking greater care of how we arrange, inhabit and treat space and do more to foster the curious relationship between productivity, memory and our visual field[4] by:

- not insisting on workplace designs that are totally

dependent on hot-desking and mandatory clear-desk policies everywhere but that enable people's minds to 'reboot' more quickly in familiar environments when they revisit a task at their desk if they need to

- providing quiet spaces where people might manage sensory overload or work quietly away from distractions and interruptions

- providing opportunities for physical exercise internally and externally in order to stimulate vestibular and proprioceptive senses

- providing food and social opportunities to stimulate olfactory and gustatory senses and the senses involved in social interaction.

Nevertheless, let us not think only about the productivity of workers but the experiences of those receiving the service from these workplaces. What are the customer experiences and the service design[5] behind the workplace? Consequently, before seeking to commission or design workplace, commercial, civic and business environments, you would do well to consult someone with appropriate mind-friendly knowledge.

32

Places of Worship

Amongst many things, places of worship are about communion –
where minds and hearts individually and collectively connect with God.

Why are you going?

If you are attending a place of worship, what is the reason that
you are attending? Could it be to find inner peace, or to use the
much deeper and broader senses of wellbeing characterized by the
Hebraic word 'shalom'? Is this not the ultimate inner state to which
we yearn?

Historic example

A favourite historic building of mine is John Wesley's New Room in
Bristol (see Figure 32.1).[1]

> This is a calm and quiet oasis in the busy central Broadmead
> shopping area of Bristol, one in which visitors may find
> at least outer peace and quiet amidst the hive of activity
> outside. It is also a place established by the man who is
> famous for having described his own encounter with inner
> peace by saying that '[as a preacher] was describing the
> change which God works in the heart through faith in Christ,
> I felt my heart strangely warmed. I felt I did trust in Christ,
> Christ alone, for salvation; and an assurance was given me

that He had taken away my sins, even mine, and saved me from the law of sin and death'.[2]

Figure 32.1 John Wesley's New Room, Bristol

Wesley and his companions would meet at various locations in the neighbourhood, until the numbers swelled to such an extent that a new room was needed. As the location of the 'first' Methodist building in the world, it has received a Grade 1 listed status. Although views out of the New Room are limited (which is a pity) daylight enters it from above – via an octagonal, lantern roof-light (inspired, it is thought, by how ocean-going passenger ships were lit). Wesley resisted having fixed pews installed, since this would have restricted access, not only to the Gospel, but to medicine and education also. Even so, pews would not have wholly stopped Wesley. By then, he was accustomed to preaching in the open air, having been persuaded of its merits by fellow preacher, George Whitfield.

It is apparent that Wesley underwent a significant shift in mind-set, once considering open-air preaching to be 'vile' but realizing that if he were to reach people, many of whom could not read, he should find ways and means of reaching out. Wesley's brother, Charles, further enabled access to the Gospel message by people who were not able to read through inspired Hymns set to popular tunes. The radical movement of the early Methodists and of similar movements reminds us that access is not solely about removing physical barriers but is about changed mind-sets, and that access and inclusion is a universal need and one that reaches the mind too.

Designing places of worship for the future

Wesley's attitude to buildings helps us to remember that there is more to a place of worship than the ceremonial and historic building perceptions that we might have. One of the important functions of places of worship is the potential they offer for enabling people to come together and to avoid becoming isolated – a human condition that is not usually conducive to people's neurological wellbeing.

However, the most significant purpose of such a space is communion, where minds and hearts individually and collectively connect with God. Psalms and other biblical scriptures, such as the one found in Isaiah 61:3, testify to the benefits of singing and music. Researchers have found that whilst people sing together, hormones associated with wellbeing increase whilst hormones associated with stress decrease.[3] It helps therefore if places of worship:

- have good acoustics

- consist of a visual environment that is relaxing to the eyes

- help our minds to reflect and meditate

- have views out.

It also helps if those who design places of worship consider the issues necessary for creating good educational,[4] music,[5] community[6] and even health and social care environments.[7]

Whilst modern places of worship (that aim to remove cultural barriers to worship) are a positive move, it is always worth taking a cautious approach to whether moves towards using multimedia, sound and visual systems are always beneficial and considering whether such technological changes can in effect lead to sensory overload if not used with moderation. For example, playing music and imagery continually in the background whilst people are speaking from the front can lead to sensory overload and make it difficult for people to process what is being said. Sometimes, therefore, it helps if worship also consists of times of quiet, stillness and waiting upon God (Psalm 46:10 and Isaiah 40:31) and that we find indoor and outdoor spaces that are conducive for quiet individual and corporate reflection. Consequently, before seeking to commission or design places of worship, you would do well to consult someone with mind-friendly knowledge.

33

Communal

Amongst many things, communal and civic environments are about community – where minds have the potential to come together.

Community and individuality

Communal environments include village halls, town halls, pubs, youth centres, churches and some external environments. As with places of worship, one of the important functions of communal and civic environments is the potential they offer for enabling people to come together and avoid becoming isolated.

As has already been stated, isolation is a human condition that is not usually conducive to people's neurological wellbeing. However, it is worth understanding that not everyone finds such environments easy to cope with and people can sometimes experience sensory overload. For this reason, it is worth considering how you might accommodate different opportunities for either social interaction or quiet individual or small-group activity within communal environments. As with other environments it is good to:

- have good acoustics[1]

- have visual environments that are relaxing on the eyes.[2]

It also makes sense to consider what makes for good food environments,[3] and landscape and urban environments,[4] where these are incorporated within a communal environment. However, before seeking to commission or design communal environments, you would be best advised to consult someone with mind-friendly knowledge.

34

Cultural and Civic

Amongst many things, cultural and civic environments such as arts, music, exhibiting and entertainment venues are about the exercise of our visual, auditory and tactile senses. But what about our other senses, and what about the relief of our senses too?

Ingredients and design opportunities

There is an obvious dynamic to arts, music, exhibiting and entertainment pertaining to engagement with people's visual, auditory and tactile senses. However, this does not necessarily equate to enjoyment, unless the sensory ingredients are conducive to the mind being able to process everything or to find relief.

When it comes to museums and exhibitions, there is quite often too much information for people to digest – causing cognitive overload and not allowing enough opportunity to rest and reflect. Alastair Somerville[1] has come to some interesting conclusions in this regard. Similar issues can surround arts, music and entertainment, and sometimes the intensity of the sensory experience is 'ramped' up to the extent that sensory overload can easily occur and enjoyment is lost. It is worth therefore considering how you might provide opportunities for people to take a break at a venue or for event organizers to incorporate breaks into their programme with sensory rest in mind. Meanwhile, it is also worth recognizing that there are opportunities to be had where designers might explore the enabling of a balanced and nourishing sensory experience.

- It goes without saying that good acoustics are a prerequisite for good cultural and civic environments. Not only are appropriate acoustics needed for given activities, a variety of acoustic environments could be provided.[2]

- Perhaps designers could also consider the visual equivalent of what goes on in acoustics and bear in mind the visual noise that can occur as a result of particular forms of lighting, colours and patterns that lead to stress. In environments where visual stimuli are not 'attuned' well, it will be a pervasive and imposing visual experience rather than an elective engagement with what is on offer.[3]

- What creative activities are on offer for all users of an environment to participate in and to exercise their senses in a restorative way? How does the environment facilitate these creative activities?

- You might also consider what other sensory experiences might be provide in conjunction with the primary sensory experiences on offer:

  - to exercise or support vestibular and proprioceptive senses through physical activity or rest in a way that blends with the exhibits, arts, music and/or entertainment on offer[4]

  - to exercise gustatory and olfactory senses through food and other aromatic opportunities in a way that also blends with the exhibits, arts, music and/or entertainment on offer, provided that the aromatic experience is not pervasive and imposed[5]

  - to provide opportunities to exercise tactile senses more purposefully[6]

  - to use natural light, views out and access to external and natural areas.[7]

- Moreover:

- What are the meanings and metaphors that people take away from their experience?[8]

- Does it make sense to them?

- Have they had time or opportunity to reflect?

It also makes sense to consider what makes for good educational,[9] community,[10] food and retail,[11] landscape and urban[12] and transport environments,[13] some or all of which may form part of the cultural or civic experience. However, before seeking to commission or design cultural and civic environments, you ought to consult someone with mind-friendly knowledge.

35

Leisure and Sports

Amongst many things, leisure and sports environments are about the exercise of our vestibular and proprioceptive senses. But what about our other senses, and what about the relief of our senses too?

Ingredients and design opportunities

There is an obvious dynamic within leisure and sports environments pertaining to engagement with people's vestibular (balance) and proprioceptive (body position) senses. However, as with the commissioning or design of cultural and civic environments, sensory exercise does not necessarily equate to enjoyment, unless the sensory ingredients are conducive to the mind being able to process everything and find relief. It might be tempting to think that physical activity is what all these environments are about. As such, it is worth considering:

- the effect that the visual environment will have on people's activity, as pervasive and imposing visual environments can affect how people function in sports and leisure pursuits[1]

- that the acoustics of sports and leisure environments can often be very reverberant and can easily lead to sensory overload and stress as a result. Consequently, it is worth considering how you might facilitate good acoustics wherever possible, quieter time-out spaces and/or quiet spectator spaces[2]

- what other sensory experiences might be provided in conjunction with the primary sensory exercises taking place during the sports and leisure activities, such as:

    - the exercise of gustatory and olfactory senses through food and other aromatic opportunities in a way that is consistent with the healthy living agenda of sports and leisure, provided that the aromatic experience is not pervasive and imposed[3]

    - opportunities to exercise the tactile senses in a way that supports the vestibular and proprioceptive senses[4]

    - the use of natural light, views out and access to external and natural areas.[5]

- Moreover, have the participants had opportunity to rest and allow their minds to reflect?

It also makes sense to consider what makes for good educational,[6] community,[7] food and drink,[8] landscape and urban[9] and transport environments,[10] some or all of which may form part of the leisure and/or sports experience. However, before seeking to commission or design leisure and sports environments, you would also be best advised to consult someone with mind-friendly knowledge.

36

Food and Drink

Amongst many things, food and drink environments, such as restaurants, canteens, cafés, pubs and bars, are about the exercise of our gustatory, olfactory, tactile and thermal senses. But are these really the only senses involved in eating?

Ingredients

As anyone who has been a parent knows, eating and drinking is far from straightforward for many children. Encouraging children to move from 'I don't like' to learning to develop an acquired taste is often a struggle.

We might think that this process is just about taste (gustatory sense) and forget that eating also involves smell (olfactory sense), touch (tactile sense) and temperature (thermal sense). Of these senses, the olfactory sense tends to be one of those senses we use to determine edibility before we eat. Furthermore, there are the tactile and thermal sensations of food held in the hand, in the mouth, on the lips or maybe on the face!

Consequently, it is not just the taste but also the smell and texture that influence whether we like something. For some people, some or all of these senses can be particularly difficult – especially when they experience hyper-sensitivity or hypo-sensitivity around any aspect of eating. As sensory processing involves the mind, it will influence how we think. However, there are other dynamics to food and drink when it comes to the mind. After all, food and drink also contain chemicals (sugars, vitamins, proteins, alcohol, caffeine, etc.) – all of which have direct or indirect impact on the brain.

Whilst it is undeniable that the gustatory, olfactory, tactile and thermal senses are the most direct senses involved in eating, let us not forget the role that the visual and auditory senses have. As with the sense of smell, we usually determine whether we are going to like something by how it looks. Our auditory sense may also be engaged by the preparation and presentation of the food or drink. We can usually tell if food is hot if it spits and crackles – or we can anticipate tea or coffee coming from sounds arising from the way it is prepared. Consequently, we could also deduce that the visual, auditory and aromatic environment in general will in some way influence our enjoyment (or otherwise) of what we are eating and drinking. The meaning and metaphors of the food and drink experience we develop will also be influenced by what we see, hear or smell and whether they add to or detract from the experience.

Andy Shipley runs Super Sense Workshops,[1] where, as a visually impaired person, he introduces people to experiencing the world without using sight. Some of his workshops centre on eating a meal without the use of sight. This enables people to concentrate on the remaining sensory signals that they have use of. For some, this will be a stimulating experience and for others it may be a particularly difficult experience – depending how their senses interact with one another. However, it does raise significant insights as to the relevance of senses beyond the immediate ones that we use in eating.

Design opportunities

There are a number of design opportunities to consider that make the activity of eating and drinking an attractive prospect in a particular place:

- Food and drink environments usually have a communal purpose, but it is worth considering how to facilitate not only large social opportunities but also small-group and individual spaces that enable people to get away from intense social stimuli.[2]

- Good acoustics are something that will be a great help for many people, as some food and drink environments give rise to intense noise and would work better if greater attention were given to attenuating noise and providing alternative spaces.[3]

- Designers could also consider toning down visual noise that can occur as a result of particular forms of lighting, colours and patterns.[4]

- You might also consider the impact that smell will have on eating:[5]

  - Could food aroma be used positively to help motivate people to eat?

  - What smells do people want to avoid?

  - How might smells be controlled?

  - Could alternative spaces be provided where aroma is not used as a stimulus should people be hyper-sensitive to certain smells?

- What are the meanings and metaphors that people take away from their experience, and what choice is there?[6]

- You might also consider what other sensory experiences could be provided in conjunction with the primary sensory experiences on offer:

  - to exercise or support vestibular and proprioceptive senses through physical activity or rest in a way that compliments the food and drink on offer[7]

  - to use natural light, views out and access to external and natural areas[8]

  - to engage children who want to exercise their other

senses (not just their gustatory senses) without noise spilling into other areas and disrupting the sensory experience of others.

It would also make sense consider what makes for good community[9] and landscape and urban environments,[10] one or both of which may form part of the food and drink experience. As with other environments, however, before seeking to commission or design food and drink environments, you would do well to consult someone with mind-friendly knowledge.

37

Retail

Amongst many things, retail environments could be about looking after someone's senses and mind so well that they want to make a purchase.

Retail is an area not unfamiliar to psychology. I once knew someone who managed a store on Oxford Street in London and doubled sales, to the amazement of her boss, by moving certain products so that they would engage people's minds just at the right time. From what we have already explored, retail will also be significantly influenced by the sensory environment and how this impacts the mind through sensory processing and integration.

Hunting, foraging and design opportunities

Some psychologists have explored hunting and foraging in retail.[1] As with hunting and foraging, in the retail environment there is a need for our minds to cope with threats and opportunities and a need for unthreatening environments that also have enough stimuli to encourage purchases. This has led store designers to take inspiration from nature and explore how product placement, design of 'unthreatening' displays and stimulating lighting design may connect with people's hunting and foraging psychology.

However, it also seems that much of retail psychology is aimed at stimulating our subconscious to do what we might have not originally planned to do. What if more attention was paid not only to product placement and active 'hunting and foraging' but to the avoidance of sensory and neurological overload? For example:

- The visual environment is going to be important:

  - The lighter and airier a store is, the less stressed a person might expect people to be. You could surmise from negative comments made by staff within buildings with no views compared to the pleasure expressed by staff in environments with daylight and views[2] that daylight and views significantly affect wellbeing and motivation, not only for staff but also customers!

  - Colour, patterns and artificial light are likely to be significant too. Getting the right balance between visual calm and visual stimulus will enable customers to navigate an environment and concentrate on purchases rather than being distracted by pervasive and intrusive visual stimuli.[3]

- The acoustic environment is going to be important too:[4]

  - Some retail stores pay little attention to acoustics and are very reverberant, leading in some cases to lots of background noise that will hardly help some people to concentrate. Furthermore, whilst background music is often used within stores, how much attention is it going to take away from the activity of purchasing items?

- Because retail stores are often large and deep-plan environments:

  - What sensory relief might you provide customers and staff?

  - How might you incorporate spaces where customers and staff alike might take sensory breaks?

  - Could such sensory break areas coincide with food, drink, views out and natural light?

- Given that children often generate a lot of noise, could there be spaces conducive to engaging children without noise spilling into the retail areas or into calm sensory break areas?

- What food and drink opportunities might there be, either connected to calm sensory break areas or apart from them?

It also makes sense to consider what makes for good community,[5] landscape and urban[6] and transport environments,[7] some or all of which may form part of the retail experience. As with other environments, before seeking to commission or design retail environments, you would also be best advised to consult someone with mind-friendly knowledge.

38

Hospitality

Amongst many things, hospitality environments should be about rest and recuperation, with an inevitable overlap with landscape and urban environments, and entertainment, leisure, health and food environments.

Sensory rest and stimulation

Unwinding, 'R and R', 'being taken care of', 'a change of scene' and 'getting away' are all descriptions that we associate with going on holiday. Where this involves staying in hotels, there is an inevitable imperative that people's minds are not only 'put at rest' but that they have the opportunity to stimulate their senses in a refreshing way. Maybe the hotel is your stopover whilst travelling on business? Even then, you will expect rest and recuperation after a long day working or travelling.

Whilst other environments have important sensory/neurological aspects to them, perhaps few other pay-to-attend environments are inherently about providing the opportunity for people's minds to find both sensory rest and stimulation. However, it would appear that many a hotel establishment forgets this. On one hand you might perceive that all that seems to matter are units of accommodation. On the other hand, you might think that designers want to show off their prowess and are in actual fact creating designs in ways that might inadvertently induce sensory stress.

Without doubt there is an element of meaning and metaphor to be had from the environments that people stay in – often taken from the locality. Maybe those commissioning the design want to demonstrate opulence and are not really sure what the design is doing to people's minds. Consequently, it is worth considering the sensory ingredients that are used to draw upon or enhance the sense of place as well.

Design criteria and opportunities

There are many design opportunities that can be explored when we consider people's diverse neurological needs within hospitality environments:

- stress-reductive acoustics – particularly in receptions and bedrooms[1]

- quiet spaces in addition to bedrooms where people can rest their senses

- visual relief out towards natural environments[2]

- activity spaces in which people can exercise their senses

- spaces designed to engage children who want to exercise their senses without noise spilling into other areas

- good wayfinding design by which people can navigate to, from and between locations.[3]

It also makes sense to consider what makes for good landscape and urban,[4] leisure and sports,[5] food and drink,[6] health,[7] civic (arts, music, exhibiting and entertainment),[8] community[9] and transport environments,[10] some or all of which may form part of the hospitality experience. However, before seeking to commission or design hospitality environments, you would also do well to consult someone with the necessary mind-friendly knowledge.

39

Industrial and Military

If nothing else, industrial and military environments should primarily be concerned with safety and security.

Critical situations

It almost goes without saying that in industrial situations, you want people's minds to be fully alert and to concentrate on the task at hand, not only for productivity reasons but in order to maintain safety. You really do not want to induce needless sensory stress into these environments and it is important also to give minds an opportunity to recuperate after intense activity.

In a similar way, in the military context you want military personnel to have minds that are fully alert and concentrated on the task at hand – especially as security as well as people's safety is at stake. However, finding rest and recuperation is perhaps that much more critical, especially after traumatic tours of duty.

It would seem that amidst occurrences of post-traumatic stress amongst military personnel, some people have minds where the sensory processing and integration is severely out of kilter and where even senses such as smell may trigger the memory of traumatic events or where vestibular and proprioceptive senses might be considered as perpetually conflicted between 'fight' and 'flight' modes to the extent that muscles are not at rest.

Design considerations and opportunities

There are basic matters to take into consideration in both industrial and military situations where personnel are in enclosed environments. These pertain to considering ways by which the sensory environment may distract from the task at hand or provide insufficient sensory relief for minds to stay attentive to the task.

What auditory, visual, olfactory, tactile vestibular and proprioceptive noises are there? Tactile vestibular and proprioceptive noises are potentially adverse vibrations and motion. To what degree does a person need to be attuned to these noises in order to be alert to what is happening, and how much might some of these noises overburden the senses and the mind?

Maybe one way of looking at specialist industrial and military environments is to consider whether there are means of adjusting the 'sensory volume' either through the treatment of the environment itself or through equipment that is handed out. Remember, it is not just for the sake of eyes or ears that these things should be considered but minds too!

Although sensory noise is a significant issue for the mind, the relief from noise and the ability for restorative processes to take place are also important. Unfortunately, industrial and some military environments are often quiet extreme. Perhaps you might therefore seriously consider opportunities for access to natural light, views and nature or, alternatively, means by which you can bring aspects of nature into an environment.[1]

When it comes to designing with post-traumatic stress in mind, though, it is also worth considering what is conducive from a health and social care environment perspective.[2] In a military context, it is particularly important to understand how access to those who have a shared experience of trauma and what it is like to be serving together under fire can be valuable. Recuperative environments can only do so much.

Before seeking to commission or design industrial and military environments you would also be best advised to consult a human factors consultancy and a registered access consultant – who will be familiar with people's neurological needs – to guide you through the design and operational considerations that pertain to a human-centric approach to these environments.

40

Judicial and Custodial

If nothing else, judicial and custodial environments should be concerned with a restorative process and not just a punitive process if they are to have lasting benefit for individuals and society.

Restorative or punitive?

It seems that when it comes to considering the design of judicial and custodial environments, designers have historically thought about security and little else. However, within the UK, a large proportion of the prison population has a mental health need.[1]

I once had the opportunity to see inside a young offender's prison as a visitor. Its design was typical of many adult prisons and was perhaps one of the most sensory-intense environments that I have visited. With lots of hard surfaces, spaces were very reverberant and noisy. Artificial lighting was fluorescent and bright and floors were shiny and reflective. External areas were basic, with little in the way of vegetation other than mown grass. It is likely that a reasonably high proportion of prisoners are going to have sensory processing difficulties as well – possibly difficulties that pertain to finding conventional education hard or sensory stress that has led to outbursts and individuals getting into trouble. Furthermore, given that some of the young offenders may have experienced childhood trauma and high levels of sensory stress, you cannot help but think that the environment cannot do much good and you wonder whether it might contribute to the build-up of stress and outbursts of violence in the prison. Consequently, such custodial environments could be unnecessarily punitive and do more harm than good. After all, if prisons are going to work in the long run, those who have been held in custody need to come out better and not worse. Indeed, the prison in question gained a poor reputation, with frequent violent episodes, and although staff made efforts to make improvements, it has ceased being used as a young offender's prison in recent years.

Other than prisons, there are arguably few more stressful places than a court building, even if their purposes are to do with civil rather than criminal law. In either form of court, emotions are likely to be running high and the last thing a person really wants to contend with in such situations is sensory stress. What is more, victims, friends, families or witnesses in a criminal case are not the guilty party and should not feel that they are being treated as such by the environment that they find themselves in. For example, I was also a witness to a violent incident on a street in Plymouth and was called to testify at a criminal court case. Whilst waiting for several hours to be called, no space was available other than a long and overheated corridor subjected to the greenhouse effect (too much glazing facing towards the sun), with a hard, wood bench to sit on. Even for a defendant, the assumption should be innocence until proven guilty and, if not considered a potential risk to others, a person should arguably have the opportunity to defend themselves in an environment that seeks to reduce as much potential sensory stress as possible. I have since had the opportunity to provide design advice pertaining to a new court building with the aim of reducing stress.

Custodial design

As with industrial and military environments, sensory noise is likely to be a problem in custodial environments, unless careful attention is paid to:

- stress-reductive acoustics, which should be applied wherever and however possible, subject to the other functional requirements that pertain to security and safety. High-level, non-combustible acoustic baffles (sound absorbent panels) in circulation and communal areas could help lower sensory stress induced by high reverberation times and noise[2]

- utilizing natural light wherever possible

- designing artificial lighting to avoid glare and flicker, and not subjecting prisoners to cool light when their body clock would expect warmer light[3]

- choosing surfaces that are not shiny so that light sources are not reflected

- using calming colours and avoiding problematic artificial patterns, so that colours and patterns neither under stimulate nor over stimulate[4]

- access to natural environments wherever possible and, failing that, views of natural environments[5]

- activity spaces in which prisoners can exercise their senses, whether that be through sports, arts or music.[6]

You might be tempted to think that such design considerations imply a soft regime for those who are in prison for punishment. However, if a custodial environment can reduce stress, then it is likely to reduce violence and be easier for staff to manage. What is more, could it be that when prisoners are released, they may be less likely to take the stress back out into the outside world and commit further crimes? When it comes to designing prisons, you might, therefore, consider what leads to better health and social care and deals with post-traumatic stress.[7]

Court design

When it comes to designing court environments, considerations could include:

- custody suites that take account of the above design considerations

- stress-reductive acoustics and visuals, particularly in public and courtroom areas

- hospitality suites for victims and also for witnesses

- family rooms

- quiet spaces where people can find respite

- views of natural environments

- activity space design in which people can exercise their senses whilst waiting

- spaces designed to engage children who want to exercise their senses without noise spilling into other areas

- good wayfinding design by which one can navigate to, from and between locations.[8]

And again, as with industrial and military environments, before seeking to commission or design judicial or custodial environments you would be best advised to consult a human factors consultancy and a registered access consultant – who will be familiar with people's neurological needs – to guide you through the design and operational considerations that pertain to a human-centric approach to these environments.

41

Domestic

Domestic environments serve multiple functions, many of which of which are found in other environment types but on a much smaller scale.

Secure and comfortable

Without getting into too much analysis or critique as to how valid Maslow's Hierarchy of Need is, it can reasonably be deduced that a sense of security is a basic need. 'An Englishman's home is his castle...', or so the saying goes. No doubt there are sayings within other cultures too. Without security, it is quite difficult to do much else but worry. Most people feel relaxed and secure if they are able to find a location from which they have the sense of refuge and prospect and can maintain defensible space and natural surveillance, all without the sense that someone will creep up behind them.[1]

Since much of that which goes on at home is sleeping, it is particularly important that an environment is conducive for sleep.[2] For this reason, and to keep away from sensory stress when awake, the avoidance of auditory noise is of significant importance.

Bear in mind that a sensory 'diet' is important, whatever our preferred diet is; exercise of our senses through interests, creativity, sports, food and drink are important aspects of our home life. As everyone has different tastes, it would be hard to stipulate what is best for people's needs other than to say that within households there may be vastly different responses to sensory stimuli. It is always worth being cognizant of what these different responses to stimuli might be, especially if members of a household have accentuated needs such as those associated with living with dementia or being on the autistic spectrum.

Applying mind-friendly landscape[3] and health and social care[4] design principles may therefore be wise where someone with higher support needs is living in a domestic setting or in their own or their family home. One might also suggest that 'retreat spaces', 'safe spaces' and outdoor 'wander spaces' are particularly important, such that bedroom and garden design become especially significant.

One of the underlying principles of the Passivhaus[5] standard, other than energy efficiency, is thermal comfort. Moreover, some of the constructional systems used to deliver Passivhaus certifiable projects tend to produce high levels of sound insulation as well. Thermal and auditory comfort go some significant way towards reducing sensory and therefore neurological stress.

Getting Serious

In this section we will look at the serious considerations
for any organization managing an environment
and how neurological needs play a part.

42

Facilities Management

Conventional wisdom would tell us that that it is essential when designing cars, ships and aircraft to consult those who drive, captain and pilot them and those who keep them operational. Yet it seems that too often, little consideration is given to this basic logic in building design!

Facilities managers often have valuable insights, but these insights frequently go unheeded. When there is a problem in the use of a building or an external environment, it will be the facilities manager to whom human resource managers, service managers and others will go to resolve the issue. Whilst options for addressing problems are limited, some facilities managers will still win a reputation for doing what they can – to the admiration of their immediate colleagues, if not their wider organization. The challenge, however, is that built environments often become 'set in stone', unable to adequately facilitate the activities that go on within them – despite the best efforts of facilities managers. How could we avoid this, or at least make sure that what is set in stone is enabling rather than disabling?

Consequently, a key question to explore and put to any project team is whether environments that facilities managers are currently managing are fit for purpose. What can be learnt? Did the designers take into account the wellbeing and inclusion of occupants, who could have benefitted from the application of foresight gained from those both using and operating such facilities?

Design for operability

No doubt facilities managers will be familiar with putting the case forward for investments in changes that bring about cost savings. Nevertheless, there is always the risk that some facilities managers could be making short-term cost savings that will have a detrimental impact on less easily quantifiable matters and erode value over the longer term, or that they overlook other changes that could yield value. As such, it is worth remembering that there are aspects of putting a value case forward rather than 'running the figures' alone.

How much better might post-occupancy outcomes be if there were prior discussion with facilities managers? What value-based insights could you bring to projects? How might you, together with facilities managers, put forward the case for early involvement in projects so that you might discuss the benefits of a more enlightened and inclusive approach for building occupants? This chapter puts forward the case for facilities managers getting in at pre-design and design stages. We could call this 'design for operability'.

Putting forward a case

Part of the issue revolves around facilities managers putting forward the case in terms that persuade not only their organization's leaders but also the project design team. This is about bringing value to what designers refer to as the brief-development stages of a project. Yes, costs and operational insight are important and indeed vital. But value to an organization is not solely derived from cost savings. Real value is much more dynamic than this. So, what do we mean by 'dynamic'? An Oxford Dictionary definition of dynamic is '(of a process or system) characterized by constant change, activity or progress'.[1] So, the definition for dynamic implies a process or system being in place.

Joined-up thinking

What so often hinders adequate brief development is narrow and blinkered thinking rather than systems thinking.[2] No one is immune from this, and whilst facilities managers are strategically placed, narrow thinking can still creep in. Let us suggest therefore that when facilities managers start looking at an issue, they break free from seeing what they do as being about process only. If they also recognize a system of interconnected subjects, then they could become the vital link. In simple terms, systems thinking is joined-up thinking 'bringing people around a table' and gathering perspectives. An example of process and system would be to use social return on investment[3] accounting principles.

Sustainability

Few business cases can now be put forward at board level without reference to sustainability. But do we really know what this means? Sustainability is not just about being environmentally responsible – it is more than this. In its simplest terms, sustainability is about being socially, economically and environmentally sustainable. This therefore starts to open up a systems-thinking approach to sustainability.

Sometimes, you might think that sustainability conveys a notion of constancy. However, change will come, and as such, sustainability thinking also means engaging with this change. We cannot always predict change, but we can start to anticipate possibilities via exploring scenarios – i.e., by applying systems thinking with a timeline.

Without a systems- and scenarios- thinking-based approach we get what we refer to as 'green badging' of environments that can in themselves be dysfunctional at a social and economic level, and hardly sustainable. So, not speaking to people-facing and economy-facing colleagues, and pointing to charts and projected environmental performance tables only, does not equate to a sustainable approach.

Resilience

For those who are keen to keep clear of disaster, you might refer to resilience as being about disaster preparedness and business recovery. However, it is not just about responding to rapid disasters but also about avoiding the attrition caused by facilities that are unresponsive to more subtle and apparently 'soft' issues, or 'slow disasters'. Slow disasters often go unnoticed and go on out of sight. These are usually the social needs that go unmet around us all the time, of which neurological needs are amongst the least visible.

Many of the challenges that facilities management are likely to encounter involve issues relating to interactions between people (whether staff, customers, clients or service users) and their facilities. On one level, facilities managers might be tempted to think of people as being the problem and what makes running the facility difficult. And yet true business value and resilience are not had from the facilities a person manages but from the people that occupy them. After all, what does 'facility' imply other than to 'facilitate' the activity of occupants?

Occupants

Even with trendy design concepts abounding, many workplace designs are not working for those who use them. People may be sold concepts such as hot-desking and clear-desk policies, but does the business know the impacts on employee wellbeing, performance and productivity? This is where a clued-up facilities manager can make sure that the right advice is sought.

One of the biggest reasons, therefore, for facilities managers getting in at the pre-design and design stages of a project is to pay proper attention to how well facilities work for their intended occupants. Human resources, equalities, customer services and therapeutic, medical, teaching and social service teams will usually have some insights, but there is a rare combination to be had in terms of the hard, technical knowledge and understanding of human factors. It is worth involving this knowledge from an early stage. Members of the National Register of Access Consultants in the UK with the necessary knowledge of people's neurological needs are amongst those with the knowledge.

Information management

It is not uncommon for built-environment and information-design projects to run separately. However, the journey for many people visiting a facility for the first time is via the information environment first. Regular users of a facility will also want to connect to the information environment within the built environment. How accessible to the mind and how usable are these information environments?

You might be inclined to think that these two environments are being integrated, as you see certain IT systems going into projects or being given as the reason for new projects. However, it is always worth taking a step back and asking some searching questions from a user-experience and service-design perspective. How will what is proposed make use of building information modelling[4]/ management to the best effect? How will an information cycle be achieved in furtherance of soft landings to improve the user experience? And what information is being put in at the beginning of the cycle to start with? This is where facilities management and their colleagues come in.

43

Safeguarding of Wellbeing

This chapter looks at the importance and relevance that layout, features and facilities have on safeguarding.

Please note: Before reading this chapter, please read the disclaimer at the beginning of this book.

Accountability

Safeguarding is where a relationship exists in which organizations and individuals are considered to be expressly accountable for the wellbeing of others. The key word to grasp here is *accountability*, as it has significant implications as to how people behave towards people for whom they are responsible. Those accountable for the wellbeing of several people at once will need to maintain both focused attention as well as peripheral attention. This can be either helped or hindered by how an environment is set out.

Wellbeing

Without an emphasis on the safeguarding of *wellbeing*, it is quite easy to lose sight of what the aim of safeguarding is and to become fixated only on preventing harm. Safeguarding should, however, imply the means by which a person remains accountable for another person's whereabouts as well.

Whereabouts

How does a person remain accountable for someone else's whereabouts, as well as their essential wellbeing, without imposing unnecessary restrictions on that person's freedoms? Some people with accentuated neurological experiences may also be vulnerable individuals with high support needs who may wander off. Consequently, a careful balance needs to be struck. Historically, and very sadly, many people have found themselves held in institutions in a manner whereby their freedoms have been severely and unnecessarily curtailed. This chapter endeavours to tackle this sensitive subject. It should also be read whilst understanding provisions of mental capacity legislation and associated deprivation of liberty safeguards.

Although matters of layout and detail will come into design, safeguarding must not be seen as just about physical characteristics of an environment, but about a joined-up approach surrounding wellbeing and accountability. Thus, previous chapters can be seen as shedding light on the safeguarding of wellbeing in addition to the following specific accountability-related considerations. The question is one of how well an environment enables accountability and wellbeing.

External threats

One of the main preoccupations for those involved in safeguarding is perceived external threats. It is quite legitimate, then, as with any working environment, to have clear means by which a person can physically prevent anyone just wandering in and out of supportive/specialist environments such as schools or care facilities without passing through a point of reception. Similarly, as with many workplaces, you will want to know when people are leaving the premises. However, it is quite easy for some individuals to wander off out of specialist premises unless there are physical and management provisions to alert staff as to when people are coming and going. Sadly, you can find two extremes. For example, it is not uncommon to find specialist environments where either all doors are locked (with no regular means of accessing safe external spaces) or where the front door is not secure or monitored and vulnerable individuals can wander off without anyone knowing.

Ironically, if there are inadequacies within the physical safeguarding features within a design, this will often lead to greater restrictions being imposed on a person through staff not wanting to 'let someone out of their sight', for fear that they may wander off and out of the premises without anybody noticing. Indeed, such close attention to someone's whereabouts is likely to lead to adverse responses. After all, how would you feel if you sensed that you were constantly under someone's supervision? In other words, if the balance is not right and the design and management are too lax, the implications will usually be counterproductive and conducive neither to someone's safety nor to their wellbeing.

Curtilages

There is a benefit to be had by designing clearly defined and understood curtilages. Usually this is best configured as front-of-house and back-of-house curtilages, where greater freedom to wander externally in back-of-house areas is possible only beyond a point of reception and where visitors can enter a front-of-house area in order to get to reception without entering back-of-house areas. Sometimes organizations such as schools will open up back-of-house areas at the beginning and end of each day only to allow interaction between parents and teachers as children are handed over. Other organizations working with people who could wander off may temporarily secure a front-of-house area when a transfer takes place between vehicles and a specialist environment.

Natural surveillance

As has been indicated, most people utilize focused and peripheral attention at the same time, especially when they have specific tasks to undertake whilst maintaining accountability for the wellbeing of others. This is in part an aspect of natural surveillance and the collective task of looking out not only for one's self but for one another. It helps therefore if environments enable us to engage our peripheral attention through appropriate layouts and sight lines. However, the success of design solutions will depend on how well tasks are divided up between focused tasks and oversight and how likely it is that particular methods of working will be maintained.

Extreme situations

It is apparent that some aspects of safeguarding may relate to 'flight' or 'fight' responses to internal and external stress triggers. The tendency for some vulnerable individuals to wander off, as described above, can be a 'flight' response to internal factors. For others, their reaction might be a 'fight' response. It must be emphasized though that many people with accentuated neurological needs do not exhibit an extreme fight response and that literal fight responses are comparatively rare. Furthermore, many of us will internalize our feelings when we become angry or agitated, which can also have implications for our health if there is no means of dealing with this. A 'fight' response can therefore be either self-harming or an expression of frustration and not necessarily literally fighting others. Even so, some individuals may become so agitated that they present a risk to themselves and those around them. This should always be borne in mind.

- Consequently: some situations may emerge simply because the environment in question is inadequate – perhaps with too many sensory triggers leading to someone becoming extremely agitated as a result. Indeed, some sensory processing and integration difficulties can be so intense that some people will experience not only stress and anxiety but pain. It is then quite easy to see why this can induce a reflex response!

- As a result, it is essential to reduce the environmental factors (such as problematic 'socially intense' spaces and poor lighting, colour, patterns, acoustics and smells) that may trigger such levels of stress and to provide choice. This might be by providing opportunities to find a positive location (internal and/or external) that a person elects to go to when they feel agitated. However, this depends on whether these spaces are available or not, and hence the need to think of what alternatives are accessible to someone before a situation becomes critical.

- When a situation does become critical, then the availability of an appropriately designed 'safe space' is vital – especially when there is a likelihood of people becoming hurt. However, such safe spaces are not cages or cells and should not be seen as such.

Safe space safeguards

- Safe spaces should only be introduced for their intrinsic therapeutic benefits so that they are spaces that individuals might readily go when they feel stressed. To duck the availability of these kinds of spaces simply because of well-meaning but poorly thought-out policies is dangerous for all concerned – especially if a risk assessment would lead to concluding that there is no alternative to providing safe spaces. However, there are some especially important principles to take into account if ever the case for such a space is to be considered:

  - If appropriately designed, safe spaces provide a means of removing or reducing sources of sensory overload that a person may feel they have no control over. Moreover, safe spaces could also be a therapeutic means by which individuals can exercise their vestibular and proprioceptive senses in safety – the senses that we sometimes want to stimulate when stressed.

  - Specialist safe spaces should never be provided in isolation of other design and management considerations aimed at either reducing stress or enabling someone to manage their own stress elsewhere in the environment.

- If they are designed correctly, they should be a space in which individuals like to be. Non-critical use of safe spaces should therefore be made available, as you do not want someone to get into a situation where the only way that they believe that they can get into that kind of space is by exhibiting the behaviour that you do not want to see happen!

- Furthermore, if there is a safe space that someone can decide to go to on their own accord, then it is much less likely to be *perceived* as a punishment if for whatever reason they find themselves taken to that space. Indeed, punishment should *never* be the motivation for having such a space; it should be a means of introducing a therapeutic facility and helping someone to manage extreme circumstances.

Design considerations:

- Safe space locations would benefit from two alternative entrances. This is about understanding an 'exit' strategy:

  - Picture an environment where, for whatever reason, someone has become so agitated that they are liable to hurt themselves and others around them.

  - What you do not want to do is reintroduce someone into that environment without some other means of breaking the pattern of events.

  - It is quite conceivable that anyone with such level of needs has an alternative trusted person in their support network and an alternative environment to go to.

  - By having another door leading to an outward-facing lobby, you can potentially provide an opportunity to break the cycle of agitation and for a handover to take place that curtails the sequence of events and provides an individual with the prospect of positive change.

- It may be that some individuals would also like to choose audible (music) or visual (images) stimuli that help them feel calm whilst in such a space. Consider therefore, an out-of-reach audio-visual means of projecting images and playing sounds. This might be pictures and sounds of natural environments (as a virtual 'view out').

- If a space is to be constructed that can be used in extreme situations:

  - Never use hard masonry surfaces.

  - Consider easily cleaned floor coverings, resilient and easy-to-compress floor backings and 'sprung floor' assemblies for walls and floors as a minimum. This then provides some impact absorption should someone be prone to self-harming.

  - Never use projecting ironmongery, external corners or another object by which someone might hang, impale or otherwise injure themselves.

  - Utilize curved internal corners and avoid sharp internal wall-to-wall and wall-to-floor corners whereby someone who is extremely distressed might inflict serious head injury by compressing their head between converging surfaces.

  - Make sure every door-to-wall surface is flush and that the door is faced with a surface similar to the walls and floors.

  - Avoid materials that can be easily ripped and used as ligature or as a means of suffocation where suicide is a risk.

  - Make sure that the ceiling is well out of reach and that light fittings are inaccessible.

  - Wherever possible use a roof light or window that is out

of reach to provide natural daylight and contact with the outside world.

However:

- The above design considerations may not be enough if someone is using a lot of energy to hurt themselves. As such, proprietary robust 'tents' may be the answer for some scenarios (see Figure 43.1):

  - They are designed with internal padded surfaces held in tension between room surfaces – providing the additional effect of a 'trampoline' surface to the floors, walls and ceilings of the tent.

  - Even so, this option may also have its limitations for some individuals in some situations.

- Always be aware that no matter what you do to mitigate and reduce harm, it is difficult and nearly impossible to prevent someone from harming themselves if they are intent on doing so. Consequently:

  - Make sure that such specialist safe spaces are adjacent to senior management so that the situation can be monitored and medical advice and/or intervention are sought if needs be.

Figure 43.1 Example of a proprietary safe space
Image provided by Safespaces

This list is not exhaustive, and any proposed solution should always be fully risk assessed according to the situation and never be implemented in isolation of carefully considered management and supervision. In other words, no one should be ever left alone in one of these spaces whilst in a stressed state, without someone looking out for their wellbeing and monitoring the situation, as the term 'safe space' is a relative term and not absolute if someone is determined to hurt themselves!

Unintended consequences

Whether or not such a safe space is provided, it remains *essential* to anticipate unintended behavioural responses from support workers and to make sure that they fully understand the management strategy for avoiding extreme situations occurring and enabling people to manage their stress levels. Support workers also need to know what other alternatives are available prior to resorting to using a specialist safe places in critical situations.

If safe spaces are used appropriately in conjunction with other strategies, they should be part of a strategy that reduces stress. In effect, if not used appropriately then you run the risk of perpetuating cyclical behaviours exhibited by both those receiving support and by those providing support. What you do not want is the presence of a specialist safe place to become the most immediate resource available in critical situations. Support workers should therefore be encouraged to explore alternative means of helping individuals manage stress and to explore the positive use of safe spaces so that they are not just used for critical situations.

Wider impacts

In some situations, proprietary safe space tents might also function as the bed in which individuals can safely get to sleep and family members might relax in the knowledge that loved ones are getting sleep whilst not coming to harm, which allows their family members to get rest as well. Such opportunities for rest and sleep should also give rise to significant behavioural benefits for all concerned.

Another important point to note about safeguarding is the implication of inadequately designed environments upon support workers and family members:

- In extreme scenarios, if you were placed in circumstances where others have accentuated neurological needs or behaviours – for which inadequate support, training and management was provided – you too could struggle to manage your mental health.

- The danger is that where support staff and family members are constantly having to manage reflex responses, their mental health can be seriously impacted without support. This is why getting the overall design right – as well as support, management and training – is so important for all concerned.

Consequently, safeguarding of wellbeing is not necessarily solely about a person with a particular need but is also about the wellbeing of those around them. This includes attention to the wider and relatively passive environmental considerations that benefit both people with accentuated neurological needs and their support workers.

44

Fire and Emergencies[1]

In this chapter we will look at some of the things you might consider when managing emergencies such as fire, where people's neurological needs ought to be taken into account.

Please note: Before reading this chapter, please read the disclaimer at the beginning of this book.

Universal benefit

There remains a potential for anybody to experience a degree of accentuated neurological need in emergency situations. This is because symptoms such as stress, anxiety and confusion are not unique to people with a known neurological difficulty. However, this should not be taken to diminish the importance of issues that can cause some people to become especially vulnerable in emergencies. In order to consider how to include people with neurological needs when planning for emergencies such as fire, it is important to take into account several issues that may be encountered.

Accentuated neurological need

Some organizations have started to understand how to respond to the needs of people with mobility, hearing and visual impairments in emergency situations, but few have begun to understand the needs of people with accentuated neurological needs. As such, many commissioners, project managers, designers and facilities managers should now start addressing these needs more adequately in their risk assessments and emergency planning. The first barrier is not the impairment of an individual but the response of others to their needs.

You would reasonably expect that staff (responsible for risk assessments and managing emergency situations) should first receive disability awareness training, including awareness of neurological impairments. More important, though, is the need to take time to consult people prior to emergency situations occurring. This information can then assist commissioners and designers in their tasks. Some people with neurological impairments may have family or key workers who can assist with consultation. However, this should not be assumed, as many people with neurological impairments will function independently. Furthermore, we are all individuals, and we are all neurologically diverse from one another. And it is not uncommon for some neurological impairment to go undiagnosed until it becomes obvious in an emergency. This is why it is important to make every effort to consult as many individuals as possible about possible adverse responses to emergency situations.

Evacuation plans

Subject to a mutual agreement, persons identified during consultations as being particularly vulnerable should be provided with a personal emergency evacuation plan (PEEP for short). This entails identifying the needs of a particular individual and how others should respond to these needs. It includes providing an individual with information, the means by which they are alerted to an emergency, the means by which they might be evacuated during an emergency and potentially includes how their needs might be attended to post-evacuation.

Where premises are open to the general public, for which there is little practical opportunity to consult individuals in advance, then it is wise to consider scenario-based, 'standard' evacuation plans that consider situations which might be reasonably anticipated.

These should be developed with the help of external consultees who have relevant experience. It may be that more than one scenario will apply, owing to people's individuality and the extent to which people can have multiple impairments (such as visual impairment and dementia or hearing impairment and autism). 'Expecting the unexpected' should also be one of the situations for which contingency provisions and processes need to adapted! Even so, most scenarios can be anticipated – even if these may be a combination of scenarios. Standard evacuation plans and some subjects for consideration are addressed in the *Government's Supplementary Guide to Fire Risk Assessments: Means of Escape for Disabled People*.[2] All these considerations can also be taken into account in the commissioning and design process.

It is in the realm of developing standard or scenario-based emergency evacuation plans that you would reasonably expect a conversation to take place between managers, commissioners and designers at the beginning of a project, whether or not there are known individuals. When consulting known individuals and planning for scenarios, helpful and important considerations are set out under the Inclusive engagement section within Chapter 6, 'For Whom or With Whom?'[3]

Planning

What does this therefore mean when considering planning for emergencies such as a fire? Communication planning perhaps more than any other issue needs to be understood, since it affects how you:

- consult an individual in order to prepare a personal emergency evacuation plan

- inform people of what the general arrangements are in the event of an emergency

- inform a person of what particular arrangements are already in place for people with particular impairments (this should not be an afterthought and should have informed the

commissioning and design processes, if the building manager
is to adequately manage their responsibilities on completion
of a project)

- alert people to an emergency situation and conduct an
  evacuation

- communicate safe evacuation routes

- account for someone's safety following an evacuation and
  any needs that might have arisen as a result of an evacuation.

When accounting for people's safety, you should seek to avoid
being over-reliant on verbal responses and make an effort to seek
to respond to certain individual's circumstances in a way that is
appropriate for them. You should also be prepared for various
responses to an emergency situation having arisen. Some people
with neurological impairments can have adverse responses to
alarms or stressful situations and may need care and assistance
during and following such eventualities.

Design and management

A number of the above considerations will influence layout,
wayfinding, signage, alarm systems and information systems within
an environment. You might therefore also consider making every
effort to ensure that:

- evacuation procedures are available in clear, simple English,
  supported by photographs or illustrations, and that
  alternative formats are available in Makaton and translated
  by a trained Makaton translator with an appropriate licence
  to use the Makaton Charity's symbols. It would usually be
  necessary for information to be clearly visible and available
  at a point of reception and also to be available as pre-arrival
  information via websites or pre-arrival posting

- arrangements are in place in order to establish the need for
  making supplementary assistance available. This is often

the task that should be facilitated by someone in reception, whether or not this is the person then charged with ensuring that a person's needs are addressed

- allowance is be made for someone having assistance for the purposes of communication or other needs:

  - If someone is a Makaton or BSL user, an interpreter and/ or symbols translator is available during consultation and the preparation of a personal emergency evacuation plan.

  - It might be that an individual does not use Makaton or BSL but might want or need other assistance when communicating their needs.

  - However, the fact that someone has an assistant should not be taken to mean that the assistant is there as someone's representative, unless this has been made clear. In other words, it is worth avoiding the 'does he take sugar?'–type question, which can easily offend an independently minded person who is able to speak for themselves!

- people are alerted to an emergency in a manner that is suited to the individual:

  - If a person has a hearing impairment, then visual alarms supported by vibrating pagers could be considered. Visual alarms alone may be inadequate or potentially problematic to other occupants of a building – unless other strategies are explored, such as the use of pagers or means of alerting fire marshals, who can then implement an appropriate management strategy to evacuate individuals.

  - Alarms need to be clearly distinguishable in order to alert a person as to what to do, should the environment be one where various sound signals indicate different responses. For example, a school environment can be one where there are different sound signals for different things. These different signals might be obvious to some, but it might be that preparation is required for others to understand different signals.

- Some people may be especially vulnerable in an emergency, as some alarms could cause them unnecessary anxiety and they may need others responsible for their support to either gently escort them to safety in a calm manner or remain with them in a place of safety.

• means of evacuating premises should be clear:

- However, this will not always be the case, even when the statutory signs have been installed 'correctly'.

- It may be that evacuation routes and procedures need to be rehearsed to engender familiarity. This might be further enhanced by colour coding, symbols or tactile-supported routes.

Some vulnerable individuals can wander off, and particular care should therefore be taken to ensure that evacuation has taken place to a location that is sufficiently secure for that person's needs or that known individuals are accompanied at all times following an evacuation. Otherwise, others might be put at risk trying to locate an individual who is assumed to be still on the premises, whilst that individual is themselves vulnerable to different hazards in an unsupervised environment. This is every support worker's nightmare in relatively straightforward circumstances, but it becomes a particular risk during emergencies. Anticipation of this scenario is therefore important, when responsibility is taken for vulnerable individuals – even if they are not known usually to wander off – as stressful situations can trigger previously unobserved responses.

Watch points

In addition to the issues that have been raised above, which are mainly ones of communication, it is worth noting that there are other particular watch points to consider. Environments that most people encounter frequently tend to have issues that are easily anticipated. Whereas some environments, owing to the activity that takes place there or the people for whom a particular environment is intended, may require a more comprehensive and all-embracing response. Some may be environments where events or industrial processes take place (which may present particular risks), or health/ social care environments where the occupants' needs would usually be known yet require understanding in terms of emergency scenarios.

The following is not an exhaustive list but raises the additional issues to be aware of when carrying out consultation and planning fire evacuation. The extent to which these issues might be prevalent, or the extent to which you can straightforwardly respond, depends on the circumstances. Some watch points that you might consider include:

- People with epilepsy can have epileptic episodes triggered by flashing lights.

    - It is important to seek specialist advice regarding flashing lights used for visual alarms and to ensure that the frequency at which they are set is such that the risk is minimized, not forgetting, though, that where there is more than one visual alarm they should be synchronized so as to avoid inadvertently raising the frequency of the flashes.

    - People with epilepsy might not consider themselves as having a cognitive impairment but consider their condition as being more physiological; however, it is apparent that whilst an epileptic episode occurs, cognitive processes can be significantly impaired and that following an epileptic episode, it may take some time to recover full cognitive function.

- It is also worth noting that it is not uncommon for some people with learning difficulties to also have epilepsy.

- Some people on the autistic spectrum can find certain sounds and/or visual stimulation problematic. Since alarms, whether visual or acoustic, are often repetitive and continuous, such signals can very rapidly lead to distress or fixation. This is thought to be because the ability to filter sensory information is impaired in those with autism. In certain situations, a point of 'overload' is easily reached, to the extent that it could be considered painful. In other situations, a person's attention can be 'locked' into the signal and become unresponsive to other stimuli.

- If there is scope to evacuate to an appropriately secure location, then this may well reduce the necessity for support workers and those managing an evacuation to have 'eyes in the back of their heads' when there is a risk of someone wandering off.

In more general environments, it may be that a support worker needs to be on hand to offer support to someone who is distressed by the means by which the alarms have been signalled or to help regain someone's attention so that they can proceed to evacuate.

The signal may be able to be reasonably adjusted to lessen the effect caused, or an alternative means of signalling an alarm can be used, such as through a voice announcement, visual displays and/ or specially trained events or venue marshals who are trained to sweep a building and marshal people to a place of safety. This can have the added advantage of lessening the scope for anxiety to occur amongst the building's population and can sometimes be the form of evacuation that is used where a large number of people are present and there is a need to avoid crowd surges. It is also a form of evacuation that you should consider where individuals are especially vulnerable, owing to the severity of their impairment(s).

Fire and emergencies summary

Carefully consider the modes and methods by which consultation, communication, alerting, wayfinding and accountability for people's whereabouts are provided before, during and after an evacuation. If you cannot remember anything else, when considering the needs of people with accentuated neurological experiences, then make sure that you remember to consult everyone, including people with accentuated neurological experiences themselves. Be prepared to communicate in a way that anticipates the communication difficulties that are probable, and seek help where necessary. Avoid singling out individuals in a manner that might make them feel uncomfortable, and make sure that consultation is a universal process involving all regular occupants of the building and all relevant external consultees. Whether or not an emergency occurs, it is often the failure of communication processes that leads to other failures occurring.

Summary

The purpose of this book has been to connect the therapeutic, medical, teaching and social world to the built-environment design/ commissioning world, and, at the same time, to help human resources, customer services, equalities and facilities managers. It is hoped that it will also empower people with a variety of neurological experiences, and/or those within their support networks, to promote mind-friendly environments and to discuss their needs with decision-makers.

Although we have looked at matters pertaining to specialist and supportive environments, this book has been about the design of environments in general to the benefit of everyone, including people with accentuated neurological experiences. It has as much relevance to public environments, civic and retail spaces and workplaces as it has to schools, hospitals and other specialist environments.

We have seen how senses play a significant role in how the mind works. These are the visual, auditory, olfactory, gustatory, tactile, vestibular, proprioceptive and interoceptive senses, added to which are the senses of deep pressure, temperature and time. We have seen how sensory noise (i.e., pervasive and uncontrollable stimuli) that we cannot control – whether auditory, visual, olfactory or thermal sensations – have an impact on our wellbeing, productivity or even recovery processes. The crucial point is that our minds need a sensory diet that we can cope with without inducing hyper-sensitive or hypo-sensitive responses. Hence design and real choices within an environment are crucial.

We have seen how environments also impact on our minds in terms of how our memories work. For example, we have identified how clearing work desks at the end of the day presents a sensory deficit in the morning and means that our brains could, as a result, take longer to 'reboot' and reconnect with our memories. We have also seen how our experiences influence our perception of the organizations that manage the environments we find ourselves in through the meanings and metaphors we develop.

As stated in the Introduction, it is not my intention that designers just create bland environments in response to this book but that they design environments that can be enjoyed by all, in which both joy and calm can be found and where the ingredients that contribute to a mind-friendly environment are orchestrated into the most elegant of architecture, interiors, landscapes and urban realms.

It has also been stated that this book has been written to help you – but it is not intended as a replacement for years of acquired knowledge: knowledge that includes an understanding of equally important physical, auditory and visual needs as well as neurological needs within the built environment. In the UK, the recognized body for accrediting access consultants is the National Register of Access Consultants. Readers are therefore strongly encouraged to engage the services of a registered access consultant with the necessary theoretical and practical knowledge of people's neurological needs.

Author Biography

Steve Maslin, RIBA, FSI, NRAC

Steve provides consultancy advice on a wide range of projects. He guests lectures, tutors and advises students as well as speaks at conferences. He also writes articles and blogs and has contributed several publications, standards and documents. Details on his activities can be found on his blog site: www.stevemaslin. wordpress.com

During his career, Steve has worked within architectural practice, housing associations, organizations working with homeless people, social services and local authority, and voluntarily within re-entry housing, social and youth projects. His work for social services involved working with adults with learning difficulties, including individuals with profound, multiple and behavioural difficulties. He has also worked as a part-time personal assistant for someone with significant mobility needs.

Steve is a Royal Institute of British Architects (RIBA) Chartered Architect, a Consultant Member of the National Register of Access Consultants (NRAC) and a Senior Research Fellow at the Schumacher Institute for Sustainable Systems. He is also a member of several British Standards Institute (BSI) committees, has held the role of Built-Environment Expert for Design Council CABE and has advised the Building Research Establishment via the BRE Global Standing Panel of Experts.

RIBA involvement via the RIBA Inclusive Design Committee included formulating representation to Government with regard to the Public Sector Equality Duty and contributing to ideas behind a series of videos produced by the RIBA. He has also served as education convenor for his local RIBA branch.

NRAC involvement includes serving on their advisory group.

BSI activities includes membership of the committee responsible for access and inclusion within the built environment (including BS8300) and membership of steering groups for several British Standards on facilities management. He has also led efforts towards design for the mind guidance and has been a steering group member for a code of practice for the recognition of dementia-friendly communities.

BRE involvement includes participation in their Planning and Communities Expert Group and providing inclusive design and social sustainability advice for the Home Quality Mark, the Code for Sustainable Homes, BREEAM Communities and other BREEAM assessment tools.

Schumacher Institute activities have included seeking to develop affordable, sustainable homes and communities. During Bristol's 2015 European Green Capital, Steve was a member of the health & wellbeing, inclusion and resilience action groups and had a particular role in developing inclusion guidelines.

Steve has also served on the Advisory Board for CHIRON (Care at Home using Intelligent Robotic Omni-functional Nodes) research and development project with Designability and Bristol Robotics Laboratory and has previously been consulted by the All-Party Parliamentary Group on Autism and the Dementia Services Development Centre in Sterling. He has also collaborated with the University of Bristol's School of Experimental Psychology's Urban Vision programme.

Because Steve both is an architect and provides specialist advice around people's needs and requirements, he has been involved in a wide range of projects: transport interchanges and urban realm; primary, secondary, tertiary and additional needs education; housing and residential; day care; supported housing; ecclesiastical; industrial and commercial; retail, leisure and sports; civic and communal; hospitality and entertainment; judicial and custodial; and health.

Steve takes particular interest in design-in-use matters, emphasizing the importance of human factors and systems thinking when clients develop project briefs, and Steve believes enabling and positive user experiences of built environments, informed by stakeholder engagement, leads to greater wellbeing, organizational effectiveness and therefore increased social, economic and environmental sustainability.

List of Figures

Figure 1.1 Models of disability 33

Figure 1.2 Collaborative or co-ability model 33

Figure 2.1 Design liable to induce trypophobia. 44

Figure 2.2 Acrophobia/vertigo-inducing view 44

Figure 2.3 Claustrophobia can influence how we respond to confined
space 45

Figure 2.4 Agoraphobia can significantly impact how we view the
prospect of external environments 45

Figure 7.1 Vitruvian Woman caricature of *Vitruvian Man*. 74

Figure 7.2 Modulor Woman caricature of *Modulor Man* 74

Figure 7.3 Aide-mémoire for the envelope of need 76

Figure 7.4 Aide-mémoire for the envelope of design 76

Figure 8.1 Stress can indicate contextual causes. 78

Figure 9.1 There are several senses 83

Figure 9.2 School chairs designed to rock 86

Figure 10.1 Is it a hole? 88

Figure 10.2 Are those steps I see? 89

Figure 10.3 Wash hand basin or urinal? 89

Figure 12.1 Warm glow of a fire 95

Figure 13.1 Anechoic chamber at Orfield Labs 101

Figure 14.1 This bridge in Bristol is known to affect people's balance . . 107

Figure 14.2 People feel dizzy with this pattern. 108

Figure 14.3 Problematic paving pattern: perception of steps, vertigo
and visual noise. 109

Figure 15.1 Mirroring reflects expression 112

Figure 15.2 The greyed-out windows at Bristol's Royal Infirmary are unfriendly, in addition to the visually noisy patterning of the fenestration. 113

Figure 15.3 Space bubbles tell us when others are too close 114

Figure 17.1 Sound separation – removing source of noise by distance . . 123

Figure 17.2 Sound insulation – reducing sound transmission between adjacent spaces. 123

Figure 17.3 Flanking sound – when sound finds a path 124

Figure 17.4 Sound attenuation – absorbing sound within a space 124

Figure 17.5 Sound reflection and reverberation – sustaining sound within a space 125

Figure 18.1 Glare- and visual noise-inducing lighting 133

Figure 19.1 High-frequency carpet pattern giving rise to visual noise . . 137

Figure 19.2 Carpet pattern with optical illusion of undulations. 137

Figure 19.3 Visually confusing floor – reflections, optical illusion and visually noisy pattern. 137

Figure 19.4 Visually busy paving pattern giving rise to visual noise. . . . 138

Figure 19.5 Visually busy mesh curtain casting visually busy shadow on floor 138

Figure 22.1 Natural patterns tend not to cause visual noise. 151

Figure 25.1 Thresholds convey privacy and dissuade uninvited entry . . 167

Figure 25.2 Defensible space does not always need to be clearly defined 167

Figure 25.3 Spaces without windows make us feel insecure. 168

Figure 25.4 Refuge – seating shielded from behind 169

Figure 25.5 Prospect – view from a vantage point 170

Figure 25.6 A random workplace nest. 171

Figure 27.1 Utilizing water to stimulate auditory senses 179

Figure 32.1 John Wesley's New Room, Bristol 194

Figure 43.1 Example of a proprietary safe space 237

References

Allman, M.J. & Meck, W.H. (2012). Pathophysiological Distortions in Time Perception and Timed Performance. *Brain, 135*(3), 656–677.

Alloway, T. P. (n.d.). *Dyslexia and Working Memory*. Retrieved on 27.05.2021 from www.psychologytoday.com/gb/blog/keep-it-in-mind/201601/dyslexia-and-working-memory

Alzheimer's Society. (n.d.-a). *Alzheimer's Society*. Retrieved on 25.04.2021 from www.alzheimers.org.uk

Alzheimer's Society. (n.d.-b). *How Do People Experience Memory Loss?* Retrieved on 25.04.2021 from www.alzheimers.org.uk/about-dementia/symptoms-and-diagnosis/symptoms/memory-loss-in-dementia

Alzheimer's Society. (n.d.-c). *Singing for the Brain*. Retrieved on 28.04.2021 from www.alzheimers.org.uk/get-support/your-support-services/singing-for-the-brain

American Occupational Therapy Association. (2008). *Frequently Asked Questions about Ayres Sensory Integration*. Retrieved on 04.25.2021 from www.aota.org/-/media/Corporate/Files/Practice/Children/Resources/FAQs/SI%20Fact%20Sheet%202.pdf

American Occupational Therapy Association. (2021). *What Is Occupational Therapy?* Retrieved on 04.25.2021 from www.aota.org/Conference-Events/OTMonth/what-is-OT.aspx

American Psychological Association. (n.d.). *Human Factors Psychology Studies Humans and Machines*. Retrieved on 25.04.2021 from www.apa.org/action/science/human-factors/index.aspx

Augustin, S. (2010, 24 December). Shopping Brings Out Our Inner Hunter/Gatherer. *Psychology Today*. Retrieved on 28.05.2021 from www.psychologytoday.com/gb/blog/people-places-and-things/201012/shopping-brings-out-our-inner-huntergatherer

BBC. (2016, 3 January). Swansea Dementia Expert Calls for Toilet Door Exit signs. *BBC*. Retrieved on 28.04.2021 from www.bbc.co.uk/news/uk-wales-34994790

Biodiversity by Design. (n.d.). *Dr Mike Wells*. Retrieved on 28.04.2021 from http://biodiversitybydesign.co.uk/people/dr-mike-wells

Birkbeck University of London. (n.d.). *Dr Alex Shepherd*. Retrieved on 25.04.2021 from www.bbk.ac.uk/psychology/our-staff/alex-shepherd

BRE Global Ltd. (2012). *BREEAM New Construction: Non-Domestic Buildings Technical Manual*. Retrieved on 28.04.2021 from www.breeam.com/ BREEAM2011SchemeDocument

Brenner, C. B. & Zacks, J. M. (2011). *Why Walking through a Doorway Makes You Forget*. Scientific American. Retrieved on 27.05.2021 from www.scientificamerican.com/article/ why-walking-through-doorway-makes-you-forget

British Dyslexia Association. (n.d.). *About the British Dyslexia Association*. Retrieved on 25.04.2021 from the British Dyslexia Association: www.bdadyslexia.org.uk/ about

Brown, N. (2001). Edward T. Hall: Proxemic Theory, 1966. *CSISS Classics, UC Santa Barbara: Center for Spatially Integrated Social Science*. Retrieved on 28.04.2021 from https://escholarship.org/uc/item/4774h1rm

Browning, W., Rya, C. & Clancy, J. (2014). *14 Patterns of Biophilic Design: Improving Health & Well-Being in the Built Environment*. Retrieved on 28.04.2021 from www.terrapinbrightgreen.com/reports/14-patterns

Brunel University London. (n.d.). *Professor Joseph Giacomin*. Retrieved on 28.04.2021 from www.brunel.ac.uk/people/joseph-giacomin

Canter, D. (1974). Underlying Dimensions. In *Psychology for Architects* (pp.76–93). London: Applied Science Publishers.

Christiansen, C. & Haertl, K. (2014). A Contextual History of Occupational Therapy. In B. Schell, G. Gillen & M. Scaffa (eds), *Willard and Spackman's Occupational Therapy* (pp.9–34). Philadelphia: Lippincott, Williams & Wilkins.

Corbett, B. A., Muscatello, R. A. & Blain, S. D. (2016). Impact of Sensory Sensitivity on Physiological Stress Response and Novel Peer Interaction in Children with and without Autism Spectrum Disorder. *Frontiers in Neuroscience, 10*, 278.

Czeisler, S. W. (2003). High Sensitivity of the Human Circadian Melatonin Rhythm to Resetting by Short Wavelength Light. *The Journal of Clinical Endocrinology & Metabolism, 88*(8), 4502–4505.

Daily Mail (n.d.). *Severely Autistic, Non-Verbal Man Stuns Public with Remarkable Singing*. Retrieved on 28.04.2021 from www.autismsupportnetwork.com/news/ severely-autistic-non-verbal-man-stuns-public-remarkable-singing-3789242

Dalke, H. (n.d.). *Hilary Dalke*. Retrieved on 28.04.2021 from www.linkedin.com/in/ hilary-dalke-02621a8

Day, K., Carreon, D. & Stump, C. (2000). The Therapeutic Design of Environments for People With Dementia: A Review of the Empirical Research. *The Gerontologist, 40*(4), 397–416. Retrieved on 25.04.2021 from https://academic. oup.com/gerontologist/article-abstract/40/4/397/641845?redirectedFrom=ful ltext

Dent, J. (2015). The Botox Dilema. *Ethics Quarterly* (99), 8–10. Retrieved on 28.04.2021 from https://search.informit.com.au/ documentSummary;dn=18573758791769;res=IELHSS

Department for Education (2015). *BB93: Acoustic Design of Schools – Performance Standards*. London: UK Government.

Donetto, S., Penfold, C., Anderson, J., Robert, G. & Maben, J. (2017). Nursing Work and Sensory Experiences of Hospital Design: A Before and After Qualitative Study Following a Move to All-Single Room Inpatient Accommodation. *Health and Place, 46*, 121–129.

Dunn, D. W. (2007). *Living Sensationally: Understanding Your Senses*. London: Jessica Kingsley Publishers.

Dyspraxia Foundation. (n.d.). *Dyspraxia Foundation*. Retrieved on 25.04.2021 from https://dyspraxiafoundation.org.uk

Electromagnetic Hypersensitivity. (n.d.) In *Wikipedia*. Retrieved on 25.04.2021 from https://en.wikipedia.org/wiki/Electromagnetic_hypersensitivity

English Oxford Living Dictionaries. (n.d.). *dynamic*. Retrieved on 28.04.2021 from https://en.oxforddictionaries.com/definition/dynamic

Epilepsy Society. (n.d.). *Facts and Statistics*. Retrieved on 25.04.2021 from www.epilepsysociety.org.uk/facts-and-statistics#.XBEq99uTLDc

Franklin, D. (2012, March 1). How Hospital Gardens Help Patients Heal. *Scientific American*. Retrieved on 25.04.2021 from www.scientificamerican.com/article/nature-that-nurtures

Gaudion, K. & McGinley, C. (2012). *Green Spaces: Outdoor Environments for Adults with Autism*. London: Helen Hamlyn Centre for Design, The Royal College of Art.

Grandin, T. (n.d.). *Temple Grandin, PhD*. Retrieved on 28.04.2021 at www.templegrandin.com

Graves, D. (2007). *John Wesley's Heart Strangely Warmed*. Retrieved on 28.04.2021 from www.christianity.com/church/church-history/timeline/1701-1800/john-wesleys-heart-strangely-warmed-11630227.html

Hauer, C. L. (n.d.). *Our Hearts in Unison with His*. Retrieved on 28.04.2021 from www.bridgesforpeace.com/letter/our-hearts-in-unison-with-his/

Henderson, A. (1974). *The Development of Sensory Integrative Theory and Practice: A Collection of the Works of A. Jean Ayres*. Dubuque, Iowa: Kendall/Hunt Pub. Co.

Horn, S. (2013, August 16). Singing Changes Your Brain. *Time*. Retrieved on 28.04.2021 from http://ideas.time.com/2013/08/16/singing-changes-your-brain

Hsin-Ni Ho, D. I. (2014). *Combining colour and temperature: A blue object is more likely to be judged aswarm than a red object*. Nature Publishing Group.

Hsu, C. (2012). *Smell 'Alarm' to Stimulate Appetite in Dementia Patients*. Medical Daily. Retrieved on 28.04.2021 from www.medicaldaily.com/smell-alarm-stimulate-appetite-dementia-patients-240266

Hull, J. M. (2016). *Touching the Rock: An Experience of Blindness*. London: SPCK Publishing.

Human Centric Lighting Society. (n.d.). Retrieved on 28.04.2021 from http://humancentriclighting.org

Johnson, M. L. (2015). The Embodied Meaning of Architecture. In S. R. Pallasmaa (ed.), *Mind In Architecture, Neuroscience, Embodiment and the Future of Design* (pp. 33–50). Cambridge, MA: The MIT Press.

Keep Calm Network (n.d.). *See Behaviour and Think Sensory*. Retrieved on 25.04.2021 from www.keepcalm-o-matic.co.uk/p/see-behaviour-and-think-sensory

Kindred, M. (2017). *Hidden Fear – Raising Awareness of How Architects, Planners and Designers Can Help Sufferers*. Kindred Games and Books. Retrieved on 27.05.2021 from http://cic.org.uk/admin/resources/hidden-fear-raising-awareness-of-how-architects-planners-and-designers-can-help-sufferers.pdf

Knight, C. & Haslam, S. A. (2010). The Relative Merits of Lean, Enriched, and Empowered Offices: An Experimental Examination of the Impact of Workspace Management Strategies on Well-Being and Productivity. *Journal of Experimental Psychology: Applied, 16*(2), 158–172.

Kolarik, A. J., Cirstea, S., Pardhan, S. & Moore B. C. J. (2014). Human Echolocation: A Summary of Research Investigating Echolocationabilities of Blind and Sighted Humans. *Hearing Research, 310*, 60–68.

KU Medical Centre. (n.d.). *Winifred (Winnie) Dunn, Ph.D., OTR, FAOTA*. Retrieved on 25.05.2021 from www.healthprofessions.missouri.edu/personnel/winnie-dunn

Larsson, J. W. (2006). Smell Your Way Back to Childhood: Autobiographical Odor Memory. *Psychonomic Bulletin & Review, 13*(2), 240–244.

Lejeune, F., Parra, J., Berne-Audéoud, F., Marcus, L., Barisnikov, K., Gentaz, E. & Debillon, T. (2016). Sound Interferes with the Early Tactile Manual Abilities of Preterm Infants. *Scientific Reports, 6*(23329). Retrieved on 27.05.2021 from www.nature.com/articles/srep23329

Lubin, G. (2014, January 22). This Heat Map Reveals the Secret to IKEA's Store Design. *Business Insider.* Retrieved on 25.04.2021 from www.businessinsider.com/this-heat-map-reveals-the-secret-to-ikeas-store-design-2014-1?r=US&IR=T

Mackie, P. (2015, May 26). Finding Their Voice: How Stroke Survivors Can Sing. *BBC News.* Retrieved on 28.04.2021 from www.bbc.co.uk/news/uk-england-birmingham-31623217

Mailloux, Z. (n.d.-a). *Innovative Designs for Engaged Attention and Learning*. Retrieved on 25.04.2021 from www.zoemailloux.com/innovative-classroom-design.html

Mailloux, Z. (n.d.-b). *Zoe Mailloux, OTD, OTR/L, FAOTA*. Retrieved on 25.04.2021 from www.zoemailloux.com

Makaton. (n.d.). *About Makaton*. Retrieved on 25.04.2021 from www.makaton.org/aboutMakaton

Mallery-Blythe, E. [Electromagnetic Health]. (2015, June 22). *Video: Erica Mallery-Blythe, MD at the Commonwealth Club of CA, June 22, 2015*. Retrieved on 25.04.2021 from Vimeo: https://vimeo.com/131798243

Mallgrave, H. F. (2015). 'Know Thyself': Or What Designers Can Learn from Contemporary Biological Sciences. In S. R. Pallasmaa (ed.), *Mind in Architecture, Neuroscience, Embodiment and the Future of Design* (pp. 9–31). Cambridge, MA: The MIT Press.

Mapes, N. (2012). Dementia Adventure, Enabling People Living with Dementia to Access Outdoor Environments. *Access by Design* (132), 9–13.

Maslin, S. (2005, Spring). A Favourite Building: The New Room, Bristol. *Access by Design*, 33.

Maslin, S. (2008). Means of Escape for People with Cognitive Impairments. in C. Fuller (ed.), *Fire and Disability 2008 – Special Report* (pp.87–92). Cambridge: Workplace Law Publishing. Retrieved on 25.04.2021, from https://books.google.co.uk/books?id=bvfxGBT9caYC&print sec=frontcover&dq=Fire+and+Disability+2008+-+Special+Report+ Workplace+Law+Network,+2008&hl=en&sa=X&ved=0ahUKEwjb5-uRqI3dAhWLyIUKHROTCMEQ6AEIKTAA#v=onepage&q=Fire%20and%20 Disability%202008%20-%20Special

Maslin, S. (2015). *Design for the Mind*. Retrieved on 25.04.2021from https://stevemaslin.wordpress.com/2015/02/06/design-for-the-mind

Maslin, S. (2017, March 27). Global Roundtable: What Are We Trying to Accomplish with Biophilic Cities? What Are Ambitious Goals and Targets, and Measures of Success? *The Nature of Cities*. Retrieved on 24.04.2021 from www.thenatureofcities.com/2017/03/27/ambitious-goals-targets-biophilic-cities-right-metrics-progress-toward-goals

Matti, J. (1997, June 8). Marion Welchman. *Independent.* Retrieved on 28.04.2021 from www.independent.co.uk/incoming/marion-welchman-5563833.html

Mencap. (n.d.). *Mencap.* Retrieved on 25.05.2021 from www.mencap.org.uk

Mental Health Foundation. (2016). *Fundamental Facts about Mental Health 2016.* Retrieved on 25.04.2021 from www.mentalhealth.org.uk/sites/default/files/fundamental-facts-about-mental-health-2016.pdf

Ministry of Housing, Communities & Local Government. (2007). *Government's Supplementary Guide to Fire Risk Assessments: Means of Escape for Disabled People.* Norwich: The Stationery Office.

Modulor. (n.d.). In *Wikipedia.* Retrieved on 25.04.2021 from https://en.wikipedia.org/wiki/Modulor

Morrell, P. (2016). *Keynote.* London: People Matter Conference: Inclusive Sustainability.

National Autisitc Society. (n.d.). *National Autistic Society.* Retrieved on 25.04.2021 from www.autism.org.uk

National Register of Access Consultants. (n.d.). *About NRAC.* Retrieved on 25.04.2021 from www.nrac.org.uk

NBS. (n.d.). *What is Building Information Modelling (BIM)?* Retrieved on 28.04.2021 from www.thenbs.com/knowledge/what-is-building-information-modelling-bim

New Economics Foundation. (n.d.). *A Guide to Social Return on Investment.* Retrieved on 28.04.2021 from https://neweconomics.org/2009/05/guide-social-return-investment

NHS. (2018). *Why Lack of Sleep Is Bad for Your Health.* Retrieved on 28.04.2021 from www.nhs.uk/live-well/sleep-and-tiredness/why-lack-of-sleep-is-bad-for-your-health

NHS Estates. (2005). *Wayfinding.* Harrogate: NHS Estates.

Northumbria University. (2016). *Herbs That Can Boost Your Mood and Memory.* Retrieved on 28.04.2021 from www.northumbria.ac.uk/about-us/news-events/news/2016/04/herbs-that-can-boost-your-mood-and-memory

Orfield, S. J. (n.d.). *Steven J. Orfield.* Retrieved on 28.04.2021 from www.linkedin.com/in/steven-j-orfield-b1a9a5

Passivhaus Trust. (n.d.) *Passivhaus Trust: The UK Passive House Organization.* Retrieved on 28.04.2021 from www.passivhaustrust.co.uk

Philpott-Robinson, K., Lane, S. J., Korostenski, L. & Lane, A. E. (2017). The Impact of the Neonatal Intensive Care Unit on Sensory and Developmental Outcomes in Infants Born Preterm: A Scoping Review. *British Journal of Occupational Therapy, 80*(8), 459–469.

Prison Reform Trust. (n.d.). *Mental Health Care in Prisons.* Retrieved on 28.04.2021 from www.prisonreformtrust.org.uk/WhatWeDo/ProjectsResearch/Mentalhealth

Rush, J. (2016). *Body Clock Wise – Lighting Design for the Circadian Cycle.* Retrieved on 28.04.2021 from www.cibsejournal.com/technical/body-clock-wise-lighting-design-for-the-circadian-cycle

Schumacher Institute. (n.d.-a) *Michael Clinton.* Retrieved on 25.04.2021 from www.schumacherinstitute.org.uk/about-us/people/core-team/?uid=michael-clinton

Schumacher Institute. (n.d.-b). *The Schumacher Institute.* Retrieved on 25.04.2021 at www.schumacherinstitute.org.uk

ScienceDaily. (2017). *Mechanisms Behind Sensory Deficits Is Parkinson's Disease*. Retrieved on 25.04.2021 from www.sciencedaily.com/releases/2017/05/170518085137.htm

Scope. (n.d.). *The Social Model of Disability*. Retrieved on 25.04.2021 from www.scope.org.uk/about-us/our-brand/social-model-of-disability

Sensory Integration Education. (n.d.-a). *Sensory Integration Education*. Retrieved on 25.04.2021 from www.sensoryintegration.org.uk

Sensory Integration Education. (n.d.-b). *Sensory Integration for Mental Health and Wellbeing*. Retrieved on 07.16.18 from www.sensoryintegration.org.uk/event-2017408

Sensory Integration Education. (n.d.-c). *What Is Sensory Integration?* Retrieved on 25.04.2021 from www.sensoryintegration.org.uk/What-is-SI

Sensory Integration Education. (n.d.-d). *Exploring the Evidence*. Retrieved on 28.12.2018 from www.sensoryintegration.org.uk: www.sensoryintegration.org.uk/Research-Exploring-the-Evidence

Service Design Network. (n.d.). *SDN Manifesto*. Retrieved on 25.04.2021 at www.service-design-network.org/manifesto

Shipley, A. (n.d.). *Super Sense Workshops*. Retrieved on 28.04.2021 from https://andyshipley-eclipse.org/supersense/

Sign Design Society. (2000). *Sign Design Guide.* London: Sign Design Society.

Solomon, P., Leiderman, P. H., Mendelson, J. & Wexler, J. (2006). Sensory Deprivation: A Review. *The American Journal of Psychiatry, 114*(4), 357–363.

Somerville, A. (n.d.) *Alastair Somerville*. Retrieved on 28.04.2021 from www.linkedin.com/in/alastair-somerville-b48b368

Stafford, T. (2012). *BBC Future Column: Why Your Brain Loves to Tune Out*. Retrieved on 28.04.2021 from https://mindhacks.com/2012/05/18/bbc-future-column-why-your-brain-loves-to-tune-out/?utm_source=twitterfeed&utm_medium=twitter

Terman, M. T. & Terman, J. S. (2005, 08). Light Therapy for Seasonal and Nonseasonal Depression: Efficacy, Protocol, Safety, and Side Effects. *CNS Spectrums, 10*(8), 647–663.

The Art of Autism. (2018). *102 Favourite Quotes About Autism and Aspergers*. Retrieved on 27.05.2021 from www.the-art-of-autism.com/favorite-quotes-about-autism-and-aspergers

The Migraine Trust. (n.d.). *Facts and Figures*. Retrieved on 25.04.2021 from www.migrainetrust.org/about-migraine/migraine-what-is-it/facts-figures

Treating reading difficulties with colour. (n.d.). Retrieved 27.05/2021 from www.bmj.com/content/349/bmj.g5160/rapid-responses

University College London. (n.d.). *Dr Nigel Oseland*. Retrieved on 28.04.2021 from www.ucl.ac.uk/bartlett/environmental-design/dr-nigel-oseland

University of Bristol. (n.d.). *Dr Ute Leonards*. Retrieved 27.05.2021 from www.bristol.ac.uk/expsych/people/ute-b-leonards/index.html

University of Essex. (n.d.). *Prof Arnold Wilkins*. Retrieved on 25.04.2021 from www.essex.ac.uk/people/wilki51608/arnold-wilkins

University of Exeter. (n.d.). *Designing Your Own Workspace Improves Health, Happiness and Productivity*. Retrieved on 25.04.2021 from www.exeter.ac.uk/news/featurednews/title_98638_en.html

Vetri, L. (2020). Autism and Migraine: An Unexplored Association? *Brain Sciences 10*(9), 615.

Vital-Durand, F., Atkinson, J. & Braddick, O. J. (1996). *Infant Vision: The European Brain and Behaviour Society Publications Series.* Oxford: Oxford University Press – Oxford Science Publications.

Vital-Durand, F., Ayzac, L. & Pinzary, G. (1996). Acuity Cards and the Search for Risk Factors in Infant Visual Development. In F. Vital-Durand, J. Atkinson & O.J. Braddick (eds), *Infant Vision: The European Brain and Behaviour Society Publications Series* (Chapter 13). Oxford: Oxford University Press – Oxford Science Publications.

Vitruvian Man. (n.d.). In *Wikipedia*. Retrieved on 25.04.2021 from https://en.wikipedia.org/wiki/Vitruvian_Man

Webster, B.J. (n.d.). *Lost and Found: Dealing with Sensory Overload after Brain Injury*. Retrieved on 25.04.2021 from www.brainline.org/article/lost-found-dealing-sensory-overload-after-brain-injury

WHO. (2005). *Electromagnetic Fields (EMF)*. Retrieved on 25.04.2021 from the World Health Organization: www.who.int/peh-emf/publications/facts/fs296/en

Wilkins, A. J. (1995). *Visual Stress*. Oxford: Oxford Medical Publications.

Wilkins, A., Penacchio, O. & Leonards, U. (2018). The Built Environment and Its Patterns: A View from the Vision Sciences. *SDAR* Journal of Sustainable Design & Applied Research, 6*(1), 42–48.

Young, R. D. (2013). Environmental Psychology Overview. In A. H. Klein (ed.), *Green Organizations: Driving Change with IO Psychology* (pp.17–33). New York: Routledge.

Endnotes

Acknowledgements
1 (University of Bristol, n.d.)

Foreword
1 (Christiansen & Haertl, 2014)
2 (American Occupational Therapy Association, 2021)
3 (American Occupational Therapy Association, 2008)

Preface
1 (Maslin, 2015)
2 (British Dyslexia Association, n.d.)
3 (Matti, 1997)
4 See Section D
5 (WHO, 2005)
6 (Mallery-Blythe, 2015)
7 (Electromagnetic Hypersensitivity, n.d.)

Introduction
1 (Schumacher Institute, n.d.-b)

Chapter 1
1 (Scope, n.d.)
2 (Mental Health Foundation, 2016)

Chapter 2
1 (National Autisitc Society, n.d.)
2 See Wellbeing or stress? in Chapter 30
3 (Henderson, 1974)
4 (Mailloux, n.d.-a)
5 (KU Medical Centre, n.d.)
6 (Dunn, 2007)
7 (Department for Education, 2015)
8 (Lejeune et al. 2016); see Application within environments in Chapter 9
9 (Vital-Durand, Ayzac & Pinzary, 1996)
10 (Alzheimer's Society, n.d.-a)
11 See Chapter 23: Time and Memory
12 (Webster, n.d.)

13 (ScienceDaily, 2017)
14 (Hull, 2016)
15 (British Dyslexia Association, n.d.)
16 (Dyspraxia Foundation, n.d.)
17 (Mencap, n.d.)
18 See Chapter 42: Facilities Management
19 (The Migraine Trust, n.d.)
20 (Epilepsy Society, n.d.)
21 (Birkbeck University of London, n.d.)
22 (Wilkins, 1995)
23 (Kindred, 2017)
24 (Mental Health Foundation, 2016)
25 (Franklin, 2012)
26 (Sensory Integration Education, n.d.-a)
27 See Chapter 43: Safeguarding of Wellbeing
28 (Day, Carreon & Stump, 2000)
29 See Chapter 43: Safeguarding of Wellbeing

Chapter 3
1 (Sensory Integration Education, n.d.-c)
2 (Sensory Integration Education, n.d.-c)
3 (Young, 2013)
4 (University of Exeter, n.d.)
5 (American Psychological Association, n.d.)
6 (Birkbeck University of London, n.d.)
7 (University of Essex, n.d.)
8 (Wilkins, Penacchio & and Leonards, 2018)
9 See Biophilia in Chapter 22
10 (Service Design Network, n.d.)
11 (National Register of Access Consultants, n.d.)

Chapter 4
1 (Philpott-Robinson, Lane, Korostenski & Lane, 2017)
2 (University of Exeter, n.d.)

3 (Department for Education, 2015)
4 (Lubin, 2014)
5 See Chapter 40 Judicial and Custodial

Chapter 5
1 See Intervention in context in Chapter 5
2 See Finding a voice in Chapter 5
3 See Finding confidence in Chapter 5
4 See Seeking allies in Chapter 5
5 See Strategy in Chapter 5
6 See Utilizing expertise in Chapter 5
7 See Project briefs in Chapter 5
8 See Proportionality in Chapter 5
9 See Engagement, co-production and service design in Chapter 6
10 (Morrell, 2016)
11 See Proportionality in Chapter 5
12 (National Register of Access Consultants, n.d.)
13 See Service design in Chapter 3
14 (The Art of Autism, 2018)

Chapter 6
1 See Models of disability in Chapter 1
2 See Project briefs in Chapter 5
3 www.confers.com
4 https://servicedesigntools.org; https://servicedesigntoolkit.org; q.health.org.uk/get-involved/creative-approaches-problem-solving-caps
5 Content drawn from the author's contribution to *Fire and Disability 2008 – Special Report* (Maslin, 2008).
6 (Makaton, n.d.)

Section B
1 (Sensory Integration Education, n.d.-c)
2 (Sensory Integration Education, n.d.-a)
3 (National Autisitc Society, n.d.)

Chapter 7
1 (Vitruvian Man, n.d.)
2 (Modulor, n.d.)
3 (Schumacher Institute, n.d.-a)

Chapter 8
1 See Section C: Contextual Experience
2 (Keep Calm Network, n.d.)
3 See Chapter 30: Health and Social Care

Chapter 9
1 See Sensory deprivation in Chapter 13
2 See Sensory overload in Chapter 13
3 See Chapter 18: Lighting; Chapter 19: Surfaces

4 See Section C: Contextual Experience
5 See Section D: Different Environments
6 (Sensory Integration Education, n.d.-c)
7 (Allman & Meck, 2012)
8 (Sensory Integration Education, n.d.-c)
9 (Sensory Integration Education, n.d.-b)
10 See Sensory deprivation in Chapter 13
11 (Dunn, 2007)
12 (Mailloux, n.d.-b)
13 (Mailloux, n.d.-a)
14 See Section C: Contextual Experience

Chapter 10
1 (Mallgrave, 2015)
2 See Mirroring and communication in Chapter 15
3 (Brunel University London, n.d.)

Chapter 11
1 See Sensory deprivation in Chapter 13
2 See Chapter 10: Emotion, Meaning and Metaphor

Chapter 12
1 (NHS, 2018)
2 See Singing and music in Chapter 17
3 See Air movement in Chapter 21
4 See Daylight and views in Chapter 22
5 See Chapter 16: Comfort and Activity
6 See Chapter 18: Lighting

Chapter 13
1 See My experience in the Preface
2 (Solomon, Leiderman, Mendelson & Wexler 2006)
3 (Orfield, n.d.)
4 (Sensory Integration Education, n.d.-d)
5 (Corbett, Muscatello & Blain 2016)
6 (Grandin, n.d.)
7 See Chapter 23: Time and Memory
8 See Chapter 20: Tastes, Smells and Air Quality
9 See Migraines, epilepsy, phobias etc. in Chapter 2

Chapter 14
1 See Chapter 17: Acoustics; Chapter 26: Communication
2 See Chapter 18: Lighting; Chapter 19: Surfaces; Chapter 22: The Natural World; Chapter 24: Navigation, Place and Wayfinding
3 See Chapter 20: Tastes, Smells and Air Quality

4   See Chapter 20: Tastes, Smells and Air Quality; Chapter 22: The Natural World
5   See Chapter 20: Tastes, Smells and Air Quality
6   See Chapter 19: Surfaces; Chapter 20: Tastes, Smells and Air Quality; Chapter 22: The Natural World; Chapter 24: Navigation, Place and Wayfinding
7   See Chapter 16: Comfort and Activity
8   See Chapter 21: Temperature
9   See Chapter 18: Lighting; Chapter 23: Time and Memory
10 See Chapter 22: The Natural World

Chapter 15
1   (Mallgrave, 2015)
2   (Dent, 2015)
3   (Mallgrave, 2015)
4   (Canter, 1974)
5   (Brown, 2001)
6   (Johnson, 2015)
7   See Security in Chapter 25

Chapter 16
1   (Mapes, 2012)
2   (Stafford, 2012)
3   (Mailloux, n.d.-a)

Chapter 17
1   (University College London, n.d.)
2   (Horn, 2013)
3   (Hauer, n.d.)
4   (Mackie, 2015)
5   (Alzheimer's Society n.d.-c)
6   (Daily Mail, n.d.)
7   (Department for Education, 2015)
8   See Sensory deprivation in Chapter 13

Chapter 18
1   (Czeisler, 2003)
2   (Allman & Meck, 2012)
3   (Vetri, L. 2020)
4   (Terman, 2005)
5   (Czeisler, 2003)
6   See Surface patterns in Chapter 19
7   (Human Centric Lighting Society, n.d.)

Chapter 19
1   (Kolarik et al., 2014)
2   (University of Essex, n.d.)
3   See Migraines, epilepsy, phobias etc. in Chapter 2
4   (University of Essex, n.d.)
5   (Dalke, n.d.)

6   (*Treating reading difficulties with colour,* n.d.)

Chapter 20
1   (Hsu, 2012)
2   (Larsson, 2006)
3   (Northumbria University, 2016)

Chapter 21
1   (Hsin-Ni Ho, 2014)

Chapter 22
1   See Chapter 14: Spatial Context
2   See Chapter 18: Lighting
3   (Terman, 2005)
4   (Czeisler, 2003)
5   See Movement in Chapter 16
6   (Browning, Rya & Clancy, 2014)
7   See Surface patterns in Chapter 19
8   (Young, 2013)
9   See Surface colour in Chapter 19
10 (Biodiversity by Design, n.d.)
11 (BRE Global Ltd., 2012)
12 (Rush, 2016)
13 Content drawn from author's contribution to 'Global Roundtable: What are we trying to accomplish with biophilic cities? What are ambitious goals and targets, and measures of success?' (Maslin, 2017).

Chapter 23
1   See Chapter 18: Lighting
2   (Allman & Meck, 2012)
3   See Chapter 20: Tastes, Smells and Air Quality
4   (Brenner & Zacks, 2011)
5   (Alloway, n.d.)
6   (Alzheimer's Society, n.d.-b)
7   See Smelling and breathing in our environment in Chapter 20
8   See Smelling and breathing in our environment in Chapter 20

Chapter 24
1   See Language, information and communication in Chapter 11
2   (BBC, 2016)
3   (Sign Design Society, 2000)
4   (NHS Estates, 2005)
5   (Makaton, n.d.)

Chapter 25
1   (Knight & Haslam, 2010)
2   See Memory in Chapter 23

3   (Somerville, n.d.)
4   See In custody in Chapter 4

Chapter 26
1   See Voice and invisibility in Chapter 1; Chapter 6: For Whom or With Whom?; Chapter 11: Reasoning, Learning and Understanding; Mirroring and communication in Chapter 15; Chapter 24: Navigation, Place and Wayfinding; Chapter 26: Communication; Information management in Chapter 42; Planning in Chapter 44

Chapter 27
1   See Chapter 14: Spatial Context
2   See Chapter 23: Time and Memory
3   See Chapter 22: The Natural World
4   See Signage in Chapter 24
5   See Chapter 25: Spatial Choice, Permission and Security
6   (Gaudion & McGinley, 2012)
7   See Surface patterns in Chapter 19; Chapter 22: The Natural World
8   See Chapter 18: Lighting
9   See Tactile surface perception in Chapter 19
10 See Chapter 17: Acoustics
11 See Chapter 16: Comfort and Activity
12 See Chapter 21: Temperature

Chapter 28
1   See Information management in Chapter 42
2   See Chapter 17: Acoustics
3   See Chapter 22: The Natural World
4   See Chapter 16: Comfort and Activity
5   See Chapter 24: Navigation, Place and Wayfinding
6   See Information management in Chapter 42

Chapter 29
1   See Chapter 16: Comfort and Activity
2   See Chapter 17: Acoustics
3   See Chapter 19 Surfaces
4   See Chapter 22: The Natural World
5   See Chapter 18: Lighting

Chapter 30
1   (Philpott-Robinson, Lane, Korostenski & Lane, 2017)
2   See Chapter 43: Safeguarding of Wellbeing

3   (Donetto, Penfold, Anderson, Robert & Maben, 2017)
4   See Chapter 17: Acoustics
5   See Chapter 18: Lighting; Surface patterns in Chapter 19; Chapter 22: The Natural World
6   See Chapter 43: Safeguarding of Wellbeing

Chapter 31
1   See Chapter 16: Comfort and Activity
2   See Chapter 17: Acoustics
3   See Chapter 18: Lighting
4   See Chapter 23: Time and Memory
5   See Service design in Chapter 3

Chapter 32
1   Content drawn from the author's contribution to 'A Favourite Building: The New Room, Bristol' (Maslin, 2005).
2   (Graves, 2007)
3   See Singing and music in Chapter 17
4   See Chapter 29: Education
5   See Chapter 34: Cultural and Civic
6   See Chapter 33: Communal
7   See Chapter 30: Health and Social Care

Chapter 33
1   See Chapter 17: Acoustics
2   See Chapter 18: Lighting; Chapter 19: Surfaces
3   See Chapter 36: Food and Drink
4   See Chapter 27: Landscape and Urban

Chapter 34
1   See Exhibitions in Chapter 25
2   See Chapter 17: Acoustics
3   See Chapter 18: Lighting; Chapter 19: Surfaces
4   See Chapter 16: Comfort and Activity
5   See Chapter 36: Food and Drink
6   See Tactile surface perception in Chapter 19
7   See Chapter 22: The Natural World
8   See Chapter 10: Emotion, Meaning and Metaphor
9   See Chapter 29: Education
10 See Chapter 33: Communal
11 See Chapter 36: Food and Drink
12 See Chapter 27: Landscape and Urban
13 See Chapter 28: Transport

Chapter 35

1 See Chapter 18: Lighting; Surface patterns in Chapter 19; Chapter 22: The Natural World
2 See Chapter 17: Acoustics
3 See Chapter 36: Food and Drink
4 See Tactile surface perception in Chapter 19
5 See Chapter 18: Lighting; Surface patterns in Chapter 19; Chapter 22: The Natural World
6 See Chapter 29: Education
7 See Chapter 33: Communal
8 See Chapter 36: Food and Drink
9 See Chapter 27: Landscape and Urban
10 See Chapter 28: Transport

Chapter 36

1 (Shipley, n.d.)
2 See Chapter 15: Social Context
3 See Chapter 17: Acoustics
4 See Chapter 18: Lighting; Surface patterns in Chapter 19
5 See Chapter 20: Tastes, Smells and Air Quality
6 See Chapter 10: Emotion, Meaning and Metaphor
7 See Chapter 16: Comfort and Activity
8 See Chapter 18: Lighting; Surface patterns in Chapter 19; Chapter 22: The Natural World
9 See Chapter 33: Communal
10 See Chapter 27: Landscape and Urban

Chapter 37

1 (Augustin, 2010)
2 See Daylight and views in Chapter 22
3 See Chapter 18: Lighting; Surface patterns in Chapter 19
4 See Chapter 17: Acoustics
5 See Chapter 33: Communal
6 See Chapter 27: Landscape and Urban
7 See Chapter 28: Transport

Chapter 38

1 See Chapter 17: Acoustics
2 See Chapter 22: The Natural World
3 See Chapter 24: Navigation, Place and Wayfinding

4 See Chapter 27: Landscape and Urban
5 See Chapter 35: Leisure and Sports
6 See Chapter 36: Food and Drink
7 See Chapter 30: Health and Social Care
8 See Chapter 34: Cultural and Civic
9 See Chapter 33: Communal
10 See Chapter 28: Transport

Chapter 39

1 See Chapter 18: Lighting; Chapter 19: Surfaces; and Chapter 22: The Natural World
2 See Chapter 30: Health and Social Care

Chapter 40

1 (Prison Reform Trust, n.d.)
2 See Chapter 17: Acoustics
3 See Chapter 18: Lighting
4 See Chapter 19: Surfaces
5 See Chapter 22: The Natural World
6 See Chapter 16: Comfort and Activity
7 See Chapter 30: Health and Social Care
8 See Chapter 24: Navigation, Place and Wayfinding

Chapter 41

1 See Chapter 25: Spatial Choice, Permission and Security
2 See Chapter 12: Rest and Sleep
3 See Chapter 27: Landscape and Urban
4 See Chapter 30: Health and Social Care
5 (Passivhaus Trust, n.d.)

Chapter 42

1 (English Oxford Living Dictionaries, n.d.)
2 See Introduction
3 (New Economics Foundation, n.d.)
4 (NBS, n.d.)

Chapter 44

1 Content drawn from the author's contribution to *Fire and Disability 2008 – Special Report* (Maslin, 2008).
2 (Ministry of Housing, Communities & Local Government, 2007)
3 See Inclusive engagement in Chapter 6

Index

access consultants 22–3, 53, 59, 62
accountability 230
acoustics
   calm environment 121–2
   components of 122–5
   psychoacoustics 119
   in schools 55
   stimulating environment 122
acrophobia 44
agoraphobia 44–5
air movement 147
air quality 105, 145
alarms 120, 133, 244–5, 246–7
allies (finding) 59–61
anechoic chamber 100, 101
anthropomorphism 88, 113
arrival information 161–2
artificial light 129–30
assistive technology 125–6
auditory perception
   of natural world 149–50
   of surfaces 134–5
auditory stimulus 104
autism 36

bars/pubs 204–7
behavioural issues (triggers for) 47, 79
bio-dynamic lighting 151
biomimicry 152
biophilia 150–2
bollard lights 131
boundaries 114–5
braille 68
brain injury 39–40

cafés 204–7
calm environments 121–2
chair design 118
childhood experiences 38–9
children's hospitals 187
choices (variation in) 113, 166
chronometric sense 3, 82
circadian rhythm 128
civic environments 199–201
claustrophobia 44–6
clear-desk policies 55
co-ability model of disability 33
co-production 66
cognitive neuroscientists 52
colour blindness 142
colours
   caution in use of 140–1
   contrast in 140, 141
   neutral background tones 141–2
   on signage 142
   theories of 139–40
   wavelengths 140
commissioning
   confidence in 59
   cost savings 58–9
   overview 57–8
   project brief 62–3
   seeking allies 59–61
   seeking proportionality 63–4
   strategy 61–2
   utilizing expertise 62
communal environments 197–8
communication
   assistive technology 125–6
   deciphering speech 120

difficulties with 67–9
digital devices 111–2
overview 173
compound neurological
    experiences 48–9
confusion (avoidance of) 88–90
context 58
cost cutting/saving 58–9, 61–2, 226
court environments 218–9
cultural environments 199–201
custodial environments 56, 172, 216–9

daylight 128–9, 148–9
deep pressure 84, 106, 249
defensible space 167
dementia
    behavioural improvements 48
    learning from 39
    maintaining familiar environments
        155
    surface patterns and 139
desks 117–8
diagnosis, dual 48–9
disability (social model) 32–3
diversity 73–6, 102–3
dizziness 107–8, 184
domestic environments 220–1
down-lighting 130
drug abuse 48
dual diagnosis 48–9
dyscalculia 41
dyslexia 41
dyspraxia 41

education environments 55, 183–5
electromagnetic hyper-
    sensitivity (EHS) 23–4
emergencies see fire and emergencies
engagement
    'fluffy' 69
    inclusive 67–9
    online resources for 66
    of stakeholders 65–6
envelope of need 75–6
environmental psychology 52
epilepsy 43, 246–7
equalities officers 59–60
evacuation plans 241–2
exhibitions 172, 199

experimental psychology 52
external lighting 131

facilities management 60, 225–9
family 49–50, 60–1
fight/flight response 233–4
fire and emergencies
    accentuated neurological
        need during 240–1
    design considerations 243–5
    evacuation plans 241–2
    planning for 242–3
    visual alarms 244–5
    watch points 246–7
flanking sound 124
flashing lights 246
food-related facilities 106, 204–7
friends 49–50
furniture
    desks 117–8
    rocking chairs 86, 117

healthcare environments
        54–5, 171, 186–9
healthcare staff 187–8
hearing impairment 40
hospitals 54–5, 171, 186–7, 188
hotels 211–2
human factors psychology 52
human resource managers 59–60

IKEA stores 56
impact of design 37
inclusive design 53
inclusive engagement 67–9
induction loops 126
industrial environments 213–5
information management 229
insulation (sound) 123
interoception 82–3
invasion of personal space 114–5
invisibility of impairment 35, 74

judicial environments 56, 216–9

language
    of architecture 92–3
    communication difficulties 67–9

language *cont.*
   divisive use of 34
   power of 31
   see also communication; terminology
learning difficulties 42–3
learning styles 38–9, 103, 183–4
leisure environments 202–3
lighting
   artificial 129–30
   background 130
   bio-dynamic 151
   external 130
   flashing 246
   natural light 128–9
   and navigation 131–2
   positioning of 130–1
   problems with 132–3
   role of 127
   transition lighting 131

Makaton 68, 163–4
medication 48
memory 154–6
mental health 46
metaphorical interpretation 87–8
migraines 43
military environments 213–5
mirroring 88, 111–2
models of disability 32–4
Modulor Man 73–4
movement 116–7
multiple chemical sensitivities
   (MCS) 23–4
museums 199
music 120–1

natural environments
   biomimicry 152
   biophilia 150–2
   design opportunities in 178–9
   implications for design 152–3
   multiple stimuli in 177–8
   smells 150
   soundscapes of 149–50
   views of 148–9
   and wellbeing 110
natural light 128–9
natural surveillance 167, 168–9, 232–3
navigation

lighting for 131–2
   see also signage; wayfinding
need, envelope of 75–6
nerve trauma/damage 39–40
neurodiversity (use of term) 33–4
neurological experiences,
   compound 48–9
New Room (Bristol) 193–5

occupational psychology 52
occupational therapy 51
offence (looking for) 31
on-arrival information 161–2
open-plan offices 55
operability 226
oxygen supply 145

path-side bollard lights 131
patterns (on surfaces) 107–9, 136–9,
   142
perception 91–2
performance envelope 75–6
permission
   custodial environments 172
   exhibitions 172
   health and social care 171
   workplaces 170–1
persona narratives 53, 66
pervasive sound 119–20
phobias 43–6, 103
physical activity 116–7
places of worship 193–6
points of reception 158, 161–2
post-traumatic stress 213
pre- and on-arrival information
   161–2
premature baby units 186–7
prison environment 56, 172, 216–9
problem-solving 58
productivity 190–1
project brief 62–3
proportionality 63–4
proprioception 82–3, 85–6, 106–9
proxemics 114–5
psychoacoustics 119
psychologically informed
   environments 189
psychology disciplines 52
pubs 204–7

repetitive sounds 120
resilience 228
rest 94–5
restaurants 204–7
retail environments 55–6, 208–10
reverberation 125
rocking chairs 86, 117

safe spaces 234–8
safeguarding
  accountability 230
  curtilages 231, 232
  external threats 231–2
  fight/flight response 233–4
  natural surveillance 167, 168–9,
    232–3
  safe spaces 234–8
schools (acoustics in) 55
seasonal affective disorder 127, 149
security 167–9, 178, 220
  see also safeguarding
senses (overview) 81–3
sensory deprivation 99–100
sensory integration theory 51
sensory integration therapy 83–4
sensory overload 101–2
sensory processing
  and integration 84–6
  theories around 83–4
  visual processing 80–1
sensory spectrum 38
service design 52–3, 65
service managers 59–60
sight impairment 40
sign language 68
signage
  colours on 142
  design of good 159–60
  multisensory needs 160–1
  pre- and on-arrival information 161–2
  symbols in 162–4
  see also wayfinding
singing 120–1
sleep 94–5
smells 105, 143–5, 150, 156
social environment 102, 111–2
social prescribing (design as) 54–6
social return on investment
    (SROI) analysis 61

sound
  absorption 124, 135
  alarms 120
  flanking details 124
  insulation 123
  pervasive 119–20
  reflection 124
  reverberation 125, 135
  separation 123
  see also acoustics
sound enhancement 125
sound field amplification system 125–6
sound paths 123
space bubbles 114–5
sports environments 202–3
spotlights 130
stairs 107–8
stakeholders 60, 65–6
standing desks 117
stimulating environments 122
stress 77–9
subjective interpretation 87–90
sunlight 128–9
support workers 49–50
surfaces
  auditory perception of 134–5
  colour of 139–42
  patterns on 107–9, 136–9, 142
  specific considerations for 141–2
  tactile perception of 135–6
surveillance (natural) 167, 168–9, 232–3
sustainability 227
systems thinking 227

tactile sense
  overview 106
  perception of surfaces 135–6
tastes 143–5
temperature 82–3, 109, 146–7
terminology 31–5
  see also language
thermal comfort 146–7
thermal sense 82–3
threshold spaces 167
time
  placing ourselves in 109–10, 154, 156
  sense of 3, 82
toilet location 158
transition lighting 131

transport environments 180–2
trypophobia 43–4

up-lighting 130
user journey 93
UX design 52–3

value engineering 61
ventilation 145
vertigo 44
vestibular sense 82–3, 85–6, 106–9
views (of outside) 148–9
visual alarms 133, 244–5
visual processing 80–1
visual stimulus 104–5
Vitruvian Man 73–4

voice
  finding 58–9
  lack of 35

walking/moving 116–7
wayfinding
  overview 157–8
  reception points 158, 161–2
  symbols in 162–4
  see also signage
welcome (feeling) 158
Wesley, John 193–5
Western culture 73–4
windows as `eyes` 168
workplaces 170–1, 190–2
worship, places of 193–6